OVER
THE
BACKYARD
WALL

For Hannah May and Julia

OVER
THE
BACKYARD
WALL

THOMAS KILROY

THE LILLIPUT PRESS
DUBLIN

First published 2018 by
THE LILLIPUT PRESS
62–63 Arbour Hill
Dublin 7, Ireland
www.lilliputpress.ie

A CIP record for this publication is available from
The British Library.

10 9 8 7 6 5 4 3 2 1

ISBN 978 1 84351 749 8

Set in 10 on 14.8 pt Baskerville by Marsha Swan
Printed in Spain by Graphy Cems

CONTENTS

It happens mostly in old age, when our personal futures close down and we cannot imagine – sometimes cannot believe in – the future of our children's children. We can't resist this rifling around in the past, sifting the untrustworthy evidence, linking stray names and questionable dates and anecdotes together, hanging on to the threads, insisting on being joined to dead people and therefore to life.

Alice Munro, *The View from Castlerock*

1

THE EYE OF MEMORY

I have been asked more than once to write a memoir and I've always had to say no, I couldn't do it. I could scarcely remember what happened the previous week, never mind the distant past, at least with any degree of accuracy. Then, in 2006, at the age of seventy-two, something odd happened to me – rather, something routine occurred – but it had an odd result. I had cataract operations in both eyes.

The new sight was remarkable in itself, as people said it would be, but the effect on my memory was startling, even unnerving. I began to see memories as something directly in front of me, not something behind in the past. These images were not in any continuous chain of happenings but in vivid shards, splinters, sometimes with missing details so that, at times, I wondered if I were losing it.

John Berger, in his beautiful little book *Cataract* (2011), describes this lack of continuity in which individual images out of the past present themselves after a cataract operation. They appear as discrete singularities. It is as if conventional, continuous narrative had been lost. I had exactly this experience myself but it was only after reading Berger that I began to understand the kind of book that I was trying to write. I have called it a memory book but I should try to explain the different approaches I have taken towards memory.

Yes, it includes a memoir of a boy growing into manhood in a small Irish town, Callan in County Kilkenny, in the years between World War II and the 1960s. But it also includes reflective passages, essay-like pages on different subjects that have a connection to the town of Callan or to my own life. This is the perspective of an elderly writer looking back upon his life and trying to fill gaps in the narrative. There is social and political history as well because this is the only way in which I could understand the place in which I found myself. The book is also about escape, self-discovery, the struggle I had to contend with the rigid culture surrounding me as a child. When I think of this escape I see the figure of a little boy, with scabby knees and bad eyesight, clambering over the backyard wall of our house in Callan and into the fair green behind it, a green place of games and play and the release of the imagination.

This is a mixed bag, indeed, but there is more. Almost everything I have written in fiction and for theatre has had a basis in history. My imagination is particularly drawn to missing details in the record, reinventing what might have been but for which there is no evidence. I have included two sections of historical fiction in this book because they supplement the other records of the past and expand my sense of pastness. It was the most natural way to convey the trauma of the town before two large invasions from without: the Cromwellian siege of the town in the seventeenth century and the German impact on the area in the aftermath of World War II. Historical fiction is another avenue of retrieval and is intimately related to memory. It is, in fact, an imaginative imitation of the process of memory. It can also provide a corrective to memory when the two are laid alongside one another as they are here. For me, this layering adds nuance and cultural depth to the book. Laid side by side, the putative facts of childhood and the fictional recreation of the past play and reflect upon one another in different ways.

There is the hazy romanticism of myself and my pals with our wooden swords playing Cromwell on Cromwell's moat in the Callan fair green. Placed beside this now is the brutal realism of the siege itself, the savagery of war and its blank indifference to the suffering of individuals. The imagination amplifies what memory has to offer. It also challenges memory. One of my discoveries in writing this book was precisely the degree of incompleteness in my own memories and the way in which my imagination kept intruding, perhaps even to the extent of creating error. Have I imagined this or did it really happen? In this way physical reality can become as evanescent as dreams.

Memory, however, also has a firm grounding in the physical. Perhaps it is the connection between memory and sight, memory and the physical eye, the actual organ of sight itself. Memories are often highly tactile, as if one can reach out and touch the remembered surfaces.

Berger gives an example of this physicality in his book: the astonishing appearance of colour, in a pristine light, after his cataract operations. In his case the dominant colour was blue. In my case the dominant colour was red. I suddenly saw, as if I were a little boy again, the deep red, painted floor of our kitchen in Callan with my mother in her apron, working away to one side.

Berger also saw his mother in her kitchen. What interests me at this point, however, is what he has to say about the connection between sight and memory. As you might expect from someone who was an expert in visual art, the analogy that he uses is of being inside a painting of Vermeer. The clarity he experiences here is a form of visual rebirth; a veil of forgetfulness is lifted and perception has been cleansed and renewed: 'The removal of cataracts is comparable with the removal of a particular form of forgetfulness. Your eyes begin to re-remember first times. And it is in this sense that what they experience after the intervention resembles a kind of visual renaissance.'

I have no idea how this very physical procedure on the eye can have such a dramatic influence on the area of the brain that controls memory. When I tried to express my confusion on this to my very patient eye doctor, she said to me that I was talking to the wrong doctor!

A cataract operation is like having a damaged limb replaced with a new one. This is what actually happens in cataract surgery: the damaged lens is replaced by a new, prosthetic one. My eye doctor assured me that the machine for calculating the adjustment of this new, man-made lens was capable of creating one with an accuracy not found in nature. I was told that I would never have to wear glasses again except when reading. Suddenly a lifetime of heavy spectacles was lifted from me. Each year the glasses became heavier and heavier. Each year the lenses were thickened in a bid to keep up with my failing sight. My nose became grooved with this weight. But even the relief from this was as nothing compared to the effect on my memory. My memory was restoring to me a physical reality that I thought had been lost for ever.

The first memory shock after the operation had this tactile physicality that was both shocking and threatening. It had to do with my right eye which was the stronger of the two. One of the traumas of any eye operation is the fear of losing one's sight. Indeed, I am sure that most people with eye problems have an inordinate sense that the eye is a particularly fragile organ, which is simply not true. It is, on the contrary, remarkably robust.

Evolutionary biologists tell us that this amazing organ is the product of hundreds of millions of years of evolution. What is striking about this evolution is that, despite the miracle of sight, the design of the eye itself is haphazard, back to front, as it were. Perhaps this is the subliminal source of our fear of injury? My fear is certainly neurotic. To this day, for instance, I cannot actually touch my eye with a finger. Contact lenses were never an option.

Here is how the American neuroscientist Stuart Firestein describes the physical process of seeing in his remarkable book *Ignorance* (2012):

> The retina, a five-layered piece of brain tissue covering the inside of the back of your eye-ball, has been dubbed a tiny brain, processing visual input in a complexly connected circuit of cells that manipulate the raw image that falls upon it from the outside world, before sending it along to higher centres of the brain for more processing until a visual perception reaches your consciousness – and all in a flash of a few dozens of milliseconds.

Perhaps because of my obsession with sight, one of the most shocking moments in theatre is the blinding of Gloucester in *King Lear*. The old man tied in the chair has his eyes plucked out in a scene of terse brutality.

I don't think I've ever seen a staging of the scene to match the terrifying impact of the language on the page. There is hysteria in the writing, the hysteria of two sadists about to feed their appetites on the destruction of the pulsing organ of sight, the 'vile jelly' of the eyeball. It would be extremely difficult to match that writing with a comparable stage action without sinking into mere sensationalism or the banal. Perhaps the nearest that I have experienced such a congruence of language and action in a production of this scene was not in Shakespeare at all but in a mechanized production of Edward Bond's play *Lear*. A machine on stage matched the horror of the language. On the other hand, the problems I have had with productions of the Shakespearean scene in the theatre may not in fact be theatrical at all but related entirely to my own obsession with the physical eye.

I was born with a squint, what, in those days, used to be called a lazy eye. The idea being that, in childhood, one eye gave up trying and the 'good' eye had to take up all the slack. The 'bad' eye, meanwhile, turned inwards in a kind of lazy, helpless surrender, a giving up of its function of looking straight ahead.

In my childhood, the home-made solution to this problem was to cover the 'good' eye with a black patch, thus forcing the 'bad' eye to sit up and take on its proper responsibilities. I have no idea whether or not this had any benefit or was even good medical practice. What I do remember was my mother stitching a black cloth cover around the right-hand lens of my heavy glasses at home in our kitchen in Callan.

I must have been six or seven years old. The brothers and sisters said I looked great. I knew I looked like a walking bad joke. Thus encumbered, I set out, wobbling, to join my pals outdoors. Those wearing spectacles were always called 'four eyes'. I can't remember the insulting name that the other boys thought up to catch this vision of myself and my black patch. Popeye?

This first memory after my operations is really about a Raleigh tricycle. As with many of these flashes of memory that I now have, there are bright colours, blues and silver and black, a beauty of metal that, even in memory, I feel I can touch in its coldness. There is also the memory smell of oil and leather, saddle and saddle bag, the pristine pedals awaiting the push of the foot, the irresistible bell on the handlebars awaiting the tinkle, the flash of the spinning wheels as this beautiful thing shot forward.

It was after Christmas and there was the run-out into the brisk open air to show off the presents from Santa Claus, the *Beano* and *Dandy* comic book annuals, a whole year of reading which, alas, we had finished before the week was out. There was the tang of the new books, the smell of glue on the spine holding together the highly illustrated covers, the odour of fresh ink, print barely dry, it seemed.

Boxed games of Ludo and Snakes & Ladders, toy trains and fire-engines, black cardboard rabbits with bow ribbons tied around their necks. Each rabbit had a stopper on its bottom. When you pulled out the stopper a flow of sweets in their coloured papers cascaded into the palm of the hand.

My best pal John Moloney got the tricycle. I never connected this glittering present to the fact that he was an only child and that there were ten of us in our house. But I remember my envy.

Heavy glasses and black eye-patch forgotten for the moment, I was up on the tricycle. I can still remember the first moment of pushing the pedal and feeling the power running through the tricycle from my feet. I'm off! To help me along, John was pushing from behind, faster and faster, one leg up on the bar between the two back wheels, one leg hopping, pushing away the ground behind him as we sped off, screeching.

Outside their house was this foot scraper, two upright metal bars with a crossbar between them like miniature rugby goal posts. You put your foot on this crossbar and scraped the dirt off the sole of your boot before entering the house.

When the front wheel hit the scraper I flew over the handle-bars. I landed face down on the scraper, one of the upright bars hitting my right eye and its patch. When I staggered up, screaming, the blood was pouring out from beneath the black patch.

There was much running and shouting so that when I stag-gered across the road towards home, holding my bloodied eye and smashed glasses, my mother was already in our front doorway, a hand to her mouth. She fainted at the sight. My mother fre-quently fainted under stress, although there were times with my father when she seemed to use this fainting as a weapon in the struggles between them. On this occasion, neighbours came running from other houses on our terrace to pick her up by the door. Someone was sent racing up the road for Dr Phelan, to see if he was in his surgery.

Glasses were glasses in those days, not plastic. Only later, as everything subsided and the eye was bared to the light, it was discovered that, in holding the broken glass in its cloth bag, my mother's black patch had saved the sight of my right eye.

2

OVER THE BACKYARD WALL

Bless 'em all, bless 'em all,
The long and the short and the tall,
Bless de Valera and Seán MacEntee,
They gave us the brown flour
And the half-ounce of tea.

I was a child of the Hitler War. That old, mocking song about efforts at wartime rationing by members of the Irish government, itself a parody of a famous World War I British army singalong march, rang through my childhood. When World War II started in September 1939 I was just a few weeks short of my fifth birthday. But, where I came from, the real news that month was not the outbreak of war but the All Ireland Hurling Final in Croke Park on the third of September between Kilkenny and Cork, the black and amber striped jerseys of Kilkenny against that vivid red of Cork.

Callan is almost on the Tipperary border, which meant that it was also on the border between two competitive hurling provinces, Leinster and Munster. On the streets of our town we lived out that old hurling rivalry between Kilkenny and Cork or Kilkenny and Tipperary. From across the Tipperary county line, the boys from Mullinahone would cycle into Callan after a Tipperary or a Cork win and raise hullabaloo in the pubs to taunt the defeated locals.

On that dark Sunday in 1939, a few days after the start of war, Kilkenny beat Cork by a single point in the All Ireland Final in Dublin. In keeping with the apocalyptic mood of the times, a severe thunderstorm broke over Croke Park in the second half of the match. It was said that Jimmy Kelly from Carrickshock took off his boots and socks and in his bare feet sent over the winning point for Kilkenny. But it was also said that few could see him through the torrential rain.

On the morning of the match the Dáil (or Irish parliament) had rushed through the Emergency Powers Act, which effectively gave Ireland its controversial neutrality in the war. In a typical Irish deployment of the English language the war years were known as The Emergency, although whose emergency exactly was never quite specified.

High up on a cement wall of a building in the centre of our town was a half-moon of lettering with the words *Callan Town Hall*. This was covered with canvas throughout the war. We children were told it was 'camouflage', to drive astray any bombers that might just happen to be passing overhead, unable to see that they were over Callan. The canvas stayed there for years after the last shot was fired, a forgotten remnant. During the war we looked nervously at the sky as we walked back and forth to the Christian Brothers School on West Street or, earlier in life, when we trooped to the Convent of Mercy School at the end of Bridge Street. Not a plane in sight.

There were ration books with detachable coupons to hand over to the shop in return for the rationed items. And there was, inevitably, black-marketeering, particularly of petrol and tea. My father was the local police sergeant. Like many policemen, he had a complex relationship with those who broke the law, a kind of intimacy, I suppose, out of a shared interest in transgression. I remember each Christmas during the war the arrival of an unexplained parcel at the house from one of the town's shopkeepers. It contained tea, sugar and other supplies. All from the black market. Payback, no question about it, to my father, but for what service he had rendered to the lawbreaker I can only guess.

My mother was a strict Catholic but, to my surprise, she had no difficulty accepting such largesse. It was one of my first encounters with the elasticity of Catholic morality, something that bothered my logical mind in childhood. There seemed to be always occasions when priests and laity could turn a blind eye to actions that were clearly questionable.

My father read the *Irish Press* newspaper each evening at the head of the kitchen table. Around the table my brothers and sisters and myself could see black arrows on simple maps on the front page of the newspaper marking the progress of armies across Europe or North Africa. The war was out there and far away.

I also remember that when we went to the matinee at the local cinema on a Saturday afternoon, the burly owner, Bill Egan, in his kiosk would (only sometimes, it has to be said) look closely at us to see who we were and then wave our few coppers away with his hand, saying, 'Pass along! Pass along!' Why we, as children of a policeman, were allowed in free remained a mystery to us. Bill was one of the town shopkeepers who could supply you with oil and petrol if you were stuck, although there were very few cars in the area at the time.

Sometimes our father listened, late at night with some of his pals, to Lord Haw Haw on the wireless. This was the nickname of William Joyce who broadcast in English for the Nazis in their elaborate propaganda machine. My father, from Galway himself, took pride in the fact that Joyce also had West of Ireland connections. As an ex-IRA man, my father had an almost natural anti-English feeling which he shared with his cronies in front of the wireless.

In the dark from our beds upstairs we children heard the nasal, mocking voice of Lord Haw Haw: 'Germany calling! Germany calling! And now this is your commentator on the news, William Joyce.'

Nearly half a century later I was to write a play, *Double Cross*, for the Field Day Theatre Company, about that voice. The play came directly out of the memory of my father and his friends loudly debating the imminent defeat of Britain downstairs in the kitchen.

Our own defenders, the Local Defence Force (LDF) and the Local Security Force (LSF), would parade on special days like St Patrick's Day. They were always accompanied by the local unit of the St John's Ambulance Brigade, led by the local chemist, Mick Bradley, all kitted out in their smart grey uniforms, with round tin helmets emblazoned with scarlet red crosses. 'Will ya look at the chamber pots on their heads!' our ample neighbour Mrs Barry would say, leaning over her front wall on Green View Terrace.

We had our brief taste of the real thing, too, when a large contingent of the Irish army camped out around the town on the way to manoeuvres by the River Blackwater in August 1942. General MacNeill and General Costello squared off before one another in a mock battle there in the one serious exercise of the army during the war. Everyone was proud of the uniforms and guns and the neat rows of tents in the fields of Westcourt outside our town, convinced that we were ready to take on anyone, Jerries, Tommies or Yanks. But it was to be another army from another time, that of Oliver Cromwell, which really took hold of my imagination as a child, staying with me to the present day. Cromwell had left his mark on that field over our backyard wall.

Callan was what used to be called a market town with somewhere between one and two thousand inhabitants. In other words, it had no indigenous industry as such but provided services for the local farming community. Indeed, I remember it as having a kind of money-free economy with a lot of ingenious improvisation going on between the mothers to get through the week, an orange ten shilling note borrowed here, a few half-crowns borrowed there.

Lines of carts, pulled by horses or donkeys, passed our front door each morning with churns of milk for the local creamery. On their way back, they carried skimmed milk for the calves at home.

My mother had a deal with a local farmer, Pat Delaney of Coolagh, where she filled a bucket from a churn of skimmed milk from his cart and occasionally bought a pound of butter at the creamery. Pat did the buying for her. She used the skimmed milk to bake delicious soda bread and currant buns and, more surprisingly, as a wash to bring up the bright red of the painted floor of our kitchen.

Behind our house at Number 4 Green View Terrace was a narrow backyard. Each of the ten houses on the terrace had one. The walls were high enough to prevent prying, so that our mother had to stand on an upturned butter box or galvanized bucket when she wanted to gossip with jolly Mrs Barry next door.

That backyard was the first place of confinement from which I had to escape. Physical places become part of our imagination as we leave them behind. When they are left behind, they take on new, imagined shapes with only a partial connection to the original. Spaces of wonder, curiosity and surprises. Spaces to be negotiated and renegotiated, walls to be climbed in the discovery of somewhere else.

If this is to be a memory book, it is also a book about a writer in his eighties playing with those memories and trying to see how this past might become usable in writing. Maybe this is another reason why fiction bleeds into the memories in this book, why I have to invent as well as remember.

I am also trying, in my final years, to make even partial sense out of personal obsessions or phobias. Top of that list would be my detestation of all things military, including the absurdity of even wearing uniforms. Is this connected to the fact that my father was a policeman?

At the end of the backyard was the outdoor lavatory, this being before we had a local sewage scheme in Callan. It was a dry lavatory with a deep pit to hold the human waste. Every so often a man came with a stinking cart to empty the cesspits behind the terrace.

Plumbing may protect us from disease. It is true that diphtheria, for instance, was endemic in the Callan of our childhood before we had a sewage scheme. Each spring came the inflamed, dreaded white spots in the throat followed by the choking, swabbing, and the roulette of tests. One negative in three tests and you found yourself in the strictly quarantined fever hospital in Kilkenny.

I have a memory of that same fever hospital, which had to do with yet another deadly infection of the time, scarlet fever (scarlatina). My memory has the selectivity of memories from childhood, a highly polished wooden floor, nothing more, with the posh smell of heavy floor polish.

The scarlet fever infection seemed to have hit our household like a wave, taking several of us at once. We children, how many I cannot remember, were standing on one side of the polished floor of the hospital with our mother, surprisingly, beside us. I say surprisingly because my memory is that she wasn't infected but had been allowed into the place to help in our care. Could this have been possible in a quarantined hospital? I have no idea but I know she was there. Across the polished floor, a great distance away, it would appear now, our father crouched upon one knee with our eldest brother standing beside him, a safe distance away from our itching bodies and inflamed faces. Our father had a brown paper bag in one hand. He took oranges, one by one, from the bag and rolled them, like a player in some exotic game, across the floor in our direction.

It must have been post-war since neither oranges nor bananas appeared in Callan until after the war. Indeed, I remember being instructed in how to peel a banana at the time, a comical fruit if ever there was one, before eating it.

Plumbing has also protected us from the constant reminder of the ramshackle, internal arrangements of the human body. There was no such protection from shit in my childhood. I can still see that cloacal man on his filthy cart, a figure out of a Dickensian nightmare, carrying away the waste from behind the terrace. Even as a child I think I had some sense of the ambiguity of his service, hovering between cleaning and reminding, doing something which no one else would do, a *memento mori* high up on a foul cart.

Over the backyard wall was the expanse of the fair green. It gave its name to Green View Terrace, where our house was, which, as the name implies, had some aspirations to gentility. The terrace stood on a hill above the town and slightly apart from it, looking down on it, as it were. In the other direction it looked away south towards the Clonmel Road and the nearby Tipperary border, with the lovely feminine, torso shape of the mountain, Slievenamon, the Mountain of the Women, lying lazily across the horizon. In truth this is not a mountain at all, rather a high dome with a cairn of stones on top that gives the appearance of a nipple on a bounteous breast.

On one occasion I remember, as a small boy, a kind of Sunday outing, a picnic hike, to this gentle, modest mountain. It was like an event out of old Russia, or a scene out of a film by Nikita Mikhalkov, a cluster of families gathering for the adventure on Green View Terrace at the workhouse gate. The women were in sun hats or scarves, with white blouses and long skirts, the men in their Sunday suits, one or two with flowers in their buttonholes, and everywhere excited, crying children, a fussing and a hugging, with squeals and shouts, reminders, advice and warnings.

About ten families were involved, with sandwiches, milk bottles and plugs of rolled newspaper as bottle stoppers, Primus stoves with their cans of paraffin to make tea for the picnic on the mountain. Bags of apples and sweets, bottles of lemonade and, maybe, something stronger for the men. Ponies and traps were loaned by local farmers for the occasion. I can see the polished wood of the traps, the iron step up and the little door with its handle at the back by which you climbed into the vehicle, the cushioned seats facing one another inside. There was nothing like this mode of transport in our daily lives on the terrace.

I remember the trap that I was in was driven by a nervous Garda Jennings from my father's police station, chosen because he was a countryman and should know about horses. There was much oohing and aahing as the pony slipped on the road passing Grace's farmyard, past the town cemetery at Kilbride and every incline between there and the village of Kilcash at the start of the climb.

We knew the great folk tale of the mountain, of course, which had given it its name, the Mountain of the Women: how the swaggering and aging giant of Irish myth, Fionn, held a race of women to the summit to decide who should be his bride. We knew the outcome, how the wily old chief contrived to have his chosen woman, Grainne, win the race through a trick. We also knew the other story of the Fenian cycle, how the old man eventually lost his bride to the handsome young Diarmuid, the pride of Fionn's own band of warriors, the Fianna.

You had to carry a stone, however small, to the summit of Slievenamon as part of your climb and add it to the cairn at the top. Happily we discovered that the mountain, so big from a distance, offered a gentle, welcoming slope, which even our small bodies could manage with the odd tumble.

I had a curious experience at one point during that outing, a typical intrusion of a child into adult affairs. Groups stopped here and there to take in the view, the great spread of fertile Tipperary land stretching away into a haze of greens and blues. I galloped into one such group, which included my mother, and knew at once that I shouldn't be there. I was already attuned to this other, adult language reserved for adult matters, which always dribbled away into silence at the approach of a child. Indeed, I think I had a partial awareness already that this was a language I had to master myself in the process of growing up. Later I learned why. It was a necessary, coded language of human secrets that I had to learn before I could become a writer.

The women were standing, pointing downhill and whispering. When I appeared, they turned together and stared at me, three or four transfixed women. They saw me but only partially. They had that dazed look of people whose minds were elsewhere, somewhere frightening. They couldn't connect that horror to the staring child in front of them, with his heavy glasses and bad eyesight. Then the moment of befuddlement was broken up and I was swept away from that place of dark mystery between the flowing female skirts.

Like so much in my childhood, I came to work out the meaning of that incident only many years later. The women had been discussing another story of the mountain, not something out of an ancient saga or folk tale, but a real event of brutal superstition, which took place at the foot of Slievenamon in a village called Ballyvadlea.

In 1895 a twenty-six-year-old woman, Bridget Cleary, was burned alive over the open fireplace of her home as a changeling, a woman possessed by the fairies. It was the last recorded incident of witchcraft in Irish history. What is particularly scarifying about the story is that Bridget was burned by her husband Michael in the company of her own relatives and neighbours. The story has attracted writers, film-makers and scholars of social history. I spent some time myself tinkering with the possibility of a play on the subject. I gave up when I realized I could not retrieve the mentality of the story. I had the narrative but not the damaged mind at its centre. I was left with crude melodrama, which would have been a failure on the stage. As I grew up and learned the full story of Bridget Cleary, I became more aware of the need to move away from such a world before I could come back to it in my imagination with some degree of composure.

The beginnings of that movement away started with the back wall of our house. Climbing over that wall into the green was for me a releasing of the imagination, an invitation to play, an escape from the everyday into a place of endless possibility. Very recently,

I came to realize that, over sixty years later, I had used that action of climbing that wall in the writing of an unproduced screenplay, 'The Colleen and the Cowboy'. I had no conscious sense that I was doing this at the time of writing, but that was what was going on.

This screenplay is set in Galway, so the scene has been moved in my imagination from one end of the country to the other. The house in the screenplay is not our house in Callan and my young hero Val is not even an alter ego of myself. His father is certainly not a portrait of my own father. But the situation is one that I lived through and the backyard wall in the script is our backyard wall of all those years ago, even if the backyard itself is different. To use something from life in fiction, you have to distort the original. Change is the beginning of invention.

Eighteen-year-old Val in the screenplay is a film buff (as I was and am myself). His playing at being a film director, directing a film of cowboys and Indians in the field behind his house, gets him into strange and ultimately life-changing adventures in the script. I remember playing such games myself with my pals on the fair green in Callan. At any rate, here is Val over the backyard wall:

EXTERIOR. BACK STREETS OF GALWAY. DAY.

Camera sweeps over narrow, cramped streets, real poverty. Rows of small, one-storey houses. A woman throwing filthy water into the street. Behind the houses a large field. VAL has set up a 'film location' in the field. He has assembled a crowd of smaller children, dressed as cowboys and Indians, all charging about while he 'directs' them. VAL wears a home-made visor and old riding britches à la the great director Erich von Stroheim. His 'camera' is also home-made, cardboard boxes, two old bicycle wheels as film reels. 'Filming' in progress.

EXTERIOR. BACKYARD OF VAL'S HOME. DAY.

An angry, rough-looking workman, VAL'S DA, comes out into the littered backyard, bits of machinery, rubbish about the place. He is followed by a cowed woman, VAL'S MA, and a scatter of small children. The DA stands on a ladder and looks into the field.

VAL'S MA (anxiously)
Is he out there?

VAL'S DA
Will ya look at that son of mine! God Almighty, what's to become of him?

EXTERIOR. FIELD. DAY.
POV VAL'S DA: VAL is still 'filming' when he and his 'cast' are shocked by his father's roar.

VAL'S DA
Get in outta there, you blitherin' eejit!

EXTERIOR. BACKYARD OF VAL'S HOME. DAY.
VAL'S DA is frog-marching VAL, still trying to hold on to the remains of his 'film camera', through the backyard.

VAL'S DA
Ye'r goin' to do a day's work, me bucko, like everywan else!

VAL'S MA
Are y'as alright, Val?

VAL'S DA (to mother)
You! 'Tis you has him the way he is!

VAL'S face: despair.

I wrote all this long before I realized where it had come from. The backyard in Callan with its escape route into play had been filed away in some corner of my brain awaiting its moment of usefulness.

There were in fact two fair greens in Callan. The one immediately behind our house was the GAA pitch for hurling matches. The lower one, closer to the town centre, was the fair green proper where the monthly Fair Day, of cattle and sheep, pigs and the odd horse, was held. This was also the place where the visiting circuses, like Duffy's or Fossett's, pitched their Big Tops. It was also the site of the annual town carnival with its dodgem cars, swing-boats and roundabouts, chair-o-planes, ghost trains and freak booths.

I vividly remember one performing act at the carnival: a small slim man in a tight black suit wearing goggles, diving from a high tower into a dangerously small tank of water. Maybe this was all the more dramatic in the darkness with spotlights from the noisy carnival generator.

The Callan Fair Day spilled out from the lower fair green, taking over the full length of Green Street in the town proper. Farmers just corralled their cattle and calves up against shop fronts and waited for the buyers to arrive in their dirty yellow butcher coats. Much yelling and spitting on palms, hand-slapping and oaths, theatrical walk-aways by the buyers and dismissal by the farmers. At this point the by-standing tangler took over. The tangler invariably looked like a tramp but his role in the beef trade was crucial. His job was to bring the two parties back together again in a deal when the deal seemed lost. At first both sides pretended elaborate indifference. There were pointed references to other, better deals up the street. But then the tangler's persuasiveness did the trick. Hands slapped as the deal was done and the tangler pocketed a few bob from each party and moved on to the next drama.

Sometimes a bullock broke free and went galumphing down the street, to the delight of myself and other small boys. I remember one of them breaking into the staid Shelley's Ladies & Gents Outfitters shop, a place of cloth smells and mysterious female combinations, now redolent of other, pungent smells of cow dung and piss, as the animal was hunted back out again and the screaming ladies closed the shop for cleaning.

There was a childhood routine that we followed with the arrival of each circus. Part of the excitement came from the early start of the routine, the first light of dawn, it seems to me now, tumbling out of bed and dressing in the dark. A line of children, we headed out the Clonmel Road, past Mrs Butler's cottage, past Grace's farmyard and the spirit house, which we knew was haunted, so we hurried our steps as we skipped by. Then, beside the wall of Kilbride Cemetery, we waited in the half-darkness until we heard the jingling and footfalls of the line of caravans and horses in the distance.

There could be nothing more exciting than the vision of that line of brightly coloured wagons, with the wild-looking circus people waving and shouting at us. Lines of piebald circus horses walked by and the odd perambulating elephant or giraffe or other exotic creature taking the air. It was like the opening of a highly coloured book there on the side of the road as we jumped and yelled, running alongside this cavalcade of promise on its way back into the lower fair green of the town.

On the GAA pitch on the upper green we learned hurling in ferocious games of 'backs and forwards'. This was a shortened version of a real match. You needed only a goalkeeper, six backs marking six forwards and two or three centre-field players out the field sending high ball after low ball into the mucky patch in front of the goal. These boys out on the field were the elegant hurlers, the kind who were sometimes referred to in my day as 'hair-oil' hurlers, hurlers, in other words, who were ostentatious masters of the Kilkenny style, wrists lifting a ball delicately on the end of the stick and sending it high into the air with the one graceful motion or sending it low and hard with fearful accuracy.

The rest of us laboured in the engine room of the backs and forwards. Fingers were sliced and heads opened in the fray. Iodine and hot water were dispensed in the backyard of our house as evening fell and my mother tut-tutted by the outside water tap at the state of our heads and hands. She had the hands and tempera-ment of a nurse as cuts, which frightened us, were quickly cleaned and bandaged and we were assured that we weren't going to die this time.

What is it about memory that makes so many days of childhood golden with sunshine? Our weather must have been as fickle then as it is today but somehow, in memory, the light and the heat persist. We certainly had hard frosts. Creeping out on a frosty night to throw a bucket of water on a slope in the street so that the next day we would run and slide, sending out sparks from our hobnailed boots. Jim Lyons yelled at us for doing this, since he had to pass the icy, slippery streak himself the next day with his horse and cart.

But what about that golden weather? Perhaps it's a matter of childhood sensuality, the feeling of touch on the skin, running in the fair green with bare feet or diving into the King's River? At such moments there is always sunshine. Then there are the more complex sensations of riding on the hay floats out to the meadows beyond the town to bring home the hay. That journey lifted the imagination.

Some of the shopkeepers in the town were also farmers, so there was a constant traffic of horses and carts from the town out to and back from the fields, bringing home the various harvests through summer into autumn. This included bringing in the hay. J.J. Dunne's workman, Ger Dermody, in his braces and belt and old hat, always let us ride on his hay float when it passed our front door.

The hay float itself was a thing of exquisite design. A flatbed, timber trailer, it rested close to the ground as it was pulled along on iron wheels. The horse reared up high above us between the shafts. The back end of the float was covered with a strip of metal, giving it a knife-edge sharpness. When we reached the meadow, the whole float was tilted at an angle and this sharp edge was pushed into the butt of the haycock. Tackle and rope embraced the bottom of the cock and Ger's magical job of pulling the cock up the incline of the float began.

This was effected by wooden arms at the front by which Ger worked the locking wheels that pulled up the cock, arm pull by arm pull. When the upright cock reached a certain point, its weight pushed the inclined float back down into its low, horizontal position with a satisfying *clock* sound of metal engaging metal. Off we went then with the stately cock of hay. On the return journey, we sat at the back on the sharp metal strip of the float, nestling into the rich dry haycock. We brought a fresh smell back into the streets of the town, like that of newly baked bread.

The American writer Katherine Anne Porter has a wonderful short story called 'The Grave'. It is one of her Miranda stories in which the nine-year-old Miranda and her twelve-year-old brother Paul are out shooting rabbits. One of the more unnerving details of the narrative is the casualness with which these American children handle guns. It is a story of a child's coming into contact with life and death in the one bundle.

Paul expertly skins and disembowels the dead rabbit under Miranda's cool gaze. That pelt will provide a fur coat for one of her dolls, although she is becoming a little bored with that particular game. When he opens the rabbit, Paul discovers the unexpected:

> Very carefully he slit the thin flesh from the centre ribs to the flanks and a scarlet bag appeared. He slit again and pulled the bag open, and there lay a bundle of tiny rabbits, each wrapped in a thin scarlet veil. The brother pulled these off and there they were, dark grey, their sleek wet down lying in minute even ripples, like a baby's head just washed, their unbelievably small delicate ears folded close, their little blind faces almost featureless.

Back in the Callan meadows when each haycock was pulled off the field, it left behind a perfectly rounded spoor of damp, blackened, decayed hay, the floor of the haycock, as it were, a ring of rot but also a place of birth. There we often found a nestling family of field mice, stirring in terror at this rude exposure to the light. The mother had fled with the lifting of the cock, and the little mice with pink mouths and claws often met their ends at the hands of schoolboys.

Did I stop from poking them with a stick? I doubt it. Children are closer than we adults are to the slime and skein of birth and, perhaps for this very reason, have Miranda's cool eye before the arrival of death. I sometimes made that return journey to the streets of Callan on the hay float, silenced and with confused feelings about the dead mice.

The fair green was one place of play, the Callan workhouse another. We were fortunate as children that one was over our backyard wall while the other was immediately opposite our front door. The workhouses dotted around the towns of Ireland were built as part of the Famine relief schemes of the mid-nineteenth century and to house the victims of famine. The remains of the buildings carry that ambiguous heritage into the present day.

In my time the Callan workhouse wall was still largely intact. A great, exterior wall fronted onto the street and encircled the whole compound, running all the way around the premises towards the open countryside, as it then was, at the back. You entered through a high, elaborate archway of cut stone facing the street. One feature of this arch was a small round stone stool to one side, perhaps, in the past, a stone for tethering horses. It had become a resting place for walkers or idlers, highly polished from its use by countless seated bums. I often sat there myself daydreaming or, as the years passed, waiting for girls to pass by.

The workhouse itself was a typical Victorian complex of buildings laid out in rows and squares. Some of the buildings were three storeys high, some two, but all were constructed of beautifully cut stone with high windows and elaborate doorways. The place was designed to accommodate six hundred paupers but often held thousands in the decades of misery and starvation before its final closure in the 1920s with the foundation of the new Irish state.

Parts of the workhouse were in such good shape that they were let out as dwellings. My best pal John Moloney, the son of another policeman, lived in one of these. It was outside this house that I had my accident with the sparkling new tricycle. You entered his house by first going through the main entrance building with its cold flagged entrance hall and large doors. It was like entering a castle. Or a fairy tale.

The Moloney home was itself part of the old workhouse residential building with high ceilings and rooms that appeared impossibly large to a child, like myself, from the cramped terrace across the road. Outside their front door was the iron foot scraper, the device that almost took my right eye out of its socket.

The rest of the workhouse was a place of mystery. Great empty dormitories, an infirmary and hospital wings, overgrown gardens and old courtyards. Sometimes, when we got in through windows, we found relics of the past, like boxes of bandages or fragments of records in old cupboards, names, dates and medical records. We had little sense of the suffering that all this debris represented.

Only later did we learn about the unmarked cemetery, Cherryfield, out the Baunta Road to which thousands of corpses were carted over the years, often, it was said, sliding off the heaped carts on the way to unmarked burial. When I was a child, people avoided Cherryfield – just an empty field with those hillocks of unidentified burials. We were told to stay away from that place. Your walk quickened and you passed by.

The open space immediately inside the front archway of the workhouse was a thicket of trees, bushes and small pathways, an overgrown jungle that became the home of our Tarzan games. First we watched the films at the Saturday matinees in Bill Egan's Gaiety Cinema down on Green Street. Then we replayed the scenes in the workhouse. I believe we saw some of the early Tarzan films with Johnny Weissmuller and Maureen O'Sullivan, such as the first *Tarzan the Ape Man*. Certainly several Tarzans flew through the air at the end of ropes suspended from the trees. I can't remember our ever having a Jane. This was strictly boys' stuff.

On as many Saturdays as we could manage, we watched the ongoing black and white serials in that cinema, serials with names like *The Devil's Circle*. Cliff-hangers every Saturday afternoon, with floods and trains out of control, maidens in distress and dashing heroes on horseback.

Kilkenny County Council used parts of the workhouse for storage, particularly for the workers repairing the roads. At some point a perfectly new steam engine split its gigantic large front roller and this damaged machine was abandoned in the jungle of the workhouse, gradually losing bits to vandals and the weather. It became a huge toy for us, a tank at war, a submarine, an aeroplane over the ocean or flying above the jungle. Anything but a broken machine, which once rolled out a newly tarred road around the town.

The workhouse gave names to one other special place in the town. Every summer when there was even the hint of sunshine, we put our swimming togs in a roll of old towel and with this bundle under our arms we headed off to the King's River. This walk took us down Chapel Lane behind the parish church until we reached the river on the west side of the town. We then followed the bank upriver, away from the town itself until we reached two swimming holes called the 'Little Paupers' and the 'Big Paupers'. One was shallow and the other had some width and depth. We were told if you learned to swim in river water, you would never drown in the sea because salt water was more buoyant than fresh water, and safer. Did we ever think, then, on our walk to the river that we were following the track of those inmates of the workhouse who were well enough to be marched with their keepers for a wash in the paupers' swimming holes, adults in one place, children in the other?

History seeped into my childhood before I could read a history book. First came the reading of the landscape and place names, a form of reading that was indelible in the way the information of a book could never be. When we asked, we were told that our town river, Avonree or the King's River, got its name from a High King of Ireland who was drowned there trying to save one of his men crossing the flooded river.

There is, in fact, an existing account of the drowning of a king, Niall Caille, in the ninth century in a river called Callainn, but whether or not this is our river is open to question. Historians point out several arguments against this explanation of the river's name or even that this was the Callain of the king's death. The point is, however, that the people believed it for generation after generation over the centuries until it reached us as children.

The tale was reinforced when we could see the way this river flooded in winter and spring. I can still remember my terror, standing on the bridge after school, and seeing my father and other policemen on a makeshift raft in the river held in place by ropes and men on either bank. They were dragging the dreaded swally hole of Powlshawn near the bridge with large hooks at the end of steel cables, for the body of a missing man. We knew from our mother, who was in a state of terror at home at these proceedings, that our father couldn't swim a stroke. Watching all this, I had no difficulty believing the story of the dead king. I could imagine his horse tumbling away in that swirling flood of white water beyond the raft with my father swaying on it.

With my laden school bag and hurley stick I walked down Green View Terrace every day, with the town hall on the right where I was to have my first experience of the stage. Past Mrs Moore's little sweet shop on the left where we bought sweets, Peggy's Leg and liquorice allsorts. That is, when we had a copper. Past Gar Freeney's milk shop opposite the garda police barracks on the right, where my father presided, past the fine courthouse on the right with the parish church to my left.

This church was known locally as the Big Chapel, perhaps to distinguish it from the Augustinian friary at the other side of the town. In time, I was to write about both churches in my novel *The Big Chapel*.

At this point Green Street in front of me plunged in a steep hill down to The Cross and the centre of Callan. This dip took me past the first of two banks, the Bank of Ireland and then the

Munster & Leinster Bank, with Bill Egan's cinema between them. On down the last dip of the street with its pubs, butchers, clothes shops, newsagents, Carey's, Dunne's, Kerwick's, and the Callan Co-op store, the one with its covered lettering during the war, to arrive, finally, at The Cross.

Until I made my First Communion, I continued on through The Cross into Bridge Street, across the bridge where I watched my father on the raft, looking out at the big moat on the other side of the bridge until I reached the Convent of Mercy School. In my day the convent was the realm of Mother Juliana, a fearsome presence for small schoolboys but in reality a woman of great vision and charity to the community.

Then at the age of seven, the Age of Reason as Catholics called it with some euphemism, the morning trek with the school bag took a different turn. I turned at The Cross with my brothers and male pals towards the all boys Christian Brothers School in West Street. The girls and smaller boys continued on their way down to the convent. It was to be the first religious segregation of the sexes, although we didn't know it at the time. The Age of Reason was also the start of the dangerous years of adolescence.

Callan had a particular connection with the Irish Christian Brothers since its founder, Edmund Ignatius Rice, was born just outside the town. In 1951 the present statue of Rice by Peter Grant was erected outside the courthouse on Green Street. My brother Paddy is immortalized there. Mr Grant was putting the finishing touches to the sculpted feet of the schoolboy figures at the side of the first Christian Brother. He asked Paddy to take off his shoes and socks, to model for the stone feet on the plinth. And so his feet are there for as long as the statue stands.

I must have presented a weedy picture of childhood, bespectacled and freckled, as I trudged back and forth to school, my insecurities leaking from my frayed cuffs. Shirts and dresses were passed down in the family from older to younger, fraying away from one to the other as they went. But, at least at the start, the clothes were always spotlessly clean. My mother did the washing in a tin bath in the back kitchen, red hands and wrists at the old washboard, with suds rising from the red carbolic soap. She watched the weather like a hawk. Two lines of washing ran the length of our backyard when the wind was right.

There is actually a contemporary description of me from those days which makes me chuckle now. In 2007 the people of Callan produced a large community book to celebrate its eight hundred years as a town. One of the contributors to the book, Father James O'Halloran, remembers seeing me as I walked home from school:

> I was actually in the same school as Thomas Kilroy for about two years but I have no clear memories of him there. I can never remember speaking to him either. I do, however, have one clear vignette of Tommy, as he was called. He was going home from school and it was his school bag that first caught my attention. It was unusually laden with books. I then turned my attention to the flaming red-haired bearer. The glasses had slid down his nose in professorial fashion and he pushed them back up. If I had known the word nerd at the time it would have fitted perfectly.

3

A NORMAN TOWN

One bright summer's day during World War II a thin, severe
neighbour, Mrs Connors, three or four doors up the terrace from
our house, sat with a group of us children in the fair green and
gave out to us because of our behaviour and our anti-English attitudes. I have this image of a woman with tight hair, a printed floral
wrap-around apron tied at the waist, hunkered down in front of
this group of schoolboys on the grass, who listened with a mixture
of devilment and astonishment to what she was saying.

   Maybe we had been playing the wrong kind of war game on
the green behind her backyard wall, Tommies and Jerries, or
shouting the wrong kinds of slogans? Maybe we had heard of
some setback for the British on the battlefields of Europe and
were shouting our approval? We certainly had no sense of the
moral issues of Nazism. And it was to be nearly twenty years
before the Jewish experience and the Holocaust would enter my
own life when I became headmaster of Stratford College, the
Jewish school in Dublin, in 1959. On the sunlit green in Callan
during the war all this knowledge was very far away from me. Jews

were people out of the Bible, dark, secretive plotters against the Lord Jesus.

The Connors had a close family association with the British army, as had many other families in the town. The cottages of the commons north of the town were particularly associated with veterans of the British army and the Royal Navy. When these soldiers came home on leave, there were frequent pitched battles on our streets, fights with local nationalists who hated anything to do with the British army. My father with his blackthorn stick and his fellow policemen, their batons waving, were kept busy then.

The severe Mrs Connors spoke to us about the war. She referred to the British army as 'our boys'. She spoke about 'our' king and the Empire and how Ireland had betrayed the cause with its craven neutrality. I seem to remember a few back-answers to her but what I most remember was her pale, angry face. It was my first encounter with the clenched presence of Irish loyalism.

Although we didn't know it at the time, Mrs Connors embodied a significant division in the country. This was an Ireland much closer to the War of Independence of 1919–21 than it was to the Ireland of today. The Ireland of today would find it very difficult to understand the cultural divisions that existed in Ireland fifty years ago. In my childhood the very mention of England and the British army was enough to start a rumpus. The division between loyalists and nationalists was also geographical. The farther west you moved on the island of Ireland, the more you would find fierce anti-English sentiment. Apart from one small Irish-speaking district south of our county, Ring, in County Waterford, you were also more likely to encounter the spoken Irish language the farther west you travelled. The most significant dividing line between east and west was the River Shannon.

Callan, on the other hand, was a Norman town, part of the more anglicized, eastern part of the country. In the Middle Ages this eastern part, mostly around Dublin, was called The Pale, defining the area that had accepted English rule and the English language. Callan was not in The Pale, as such, but it might as well have been.

It was granted a charter in 1207 by the Norman baron William Marshall the Elder, Earl of Pembroke. He was one of the leading Norman nobles of his time, having great estates in the Marches of Wales, in England and France, as well as in Ireland. He had a manor house in Callan. The whole county of Kilkenny around Callan was parcelled out among his household knights, fitz Robert, fitz Anthony, de Erlee, de Hamtonsford with the lesser names Grace, St Leger, Devereux occupying more modest seats.

The Normans brought with them their genius for town planning and administration, which is reflected in the layout of Callan, its four streets laid out like the arms of a compass, with the crossroads, known locally as The Cross, at its centre. The Norman rule of law and sense of property and use of money also affected the culture of the town. Callan acquired a corporation, a sovereign or mayor, a town mace and its sergeant-at-mace, a number of burgesses and freemen who met in the Tholsel, which also housed the local court.

The figure of the single Norman knight, plated in armour, a one-man tank, transformed warfare across northern Europe, an early introduction of technology to the old game of war. The sight of such a figure, with his few attendants, must have terrified the native Irish fighters, reliant on light weapons and speedy feet across difficult terrain. The Norman place-names around Callan, Mallardstown and Earlstown ring with the chink of chainmail and the echoes of falling metal helmets and shields.

In time, Callan became a walled town and these walls awaited the arrival of Cromwell in 1650, another great wave of English invasion to hit the area, followed by a similar wave of settlers with strange names who moved into the town and countryside when the natives were moved out and towards the west. Like all Kilkenny County, Callan had followed the Royalist cause in the Civil War. The Cromwellians destroyed the town on their passage to Kilkenny city.

I think of this history of anglicization as I think of pale Mrs Connors sitting on the grass of the fair green of Callan, talking about King and Country and 'our boys' fighting the war. My own people had come from a different Ireland, with different allegiances.

My mother and father were both from west of the River Shannon. In some respects, this made them outsiders all their lives in the Norman fastnesses of County Kilkenny, and this distinction was passed on in palpable fashion to us children. As children, we had one foot in another Ireland that was very different to that of Callan.

Every summer of our childhood we were packed off westward to the uncles and aunts in County Galway. We travelled by bus and train through Kilkenny, changing platforms at Portarlington, crossing the River Shannon at Athlone and finally arriving at the little station of Woodlawn. There we were met by a relative, Paddy Mannion, with his polished sidecar. The beautiful roan mare galloped off up the incline from the station, carrying our suitcases and us, giddily clinging to the high leather seats, into the dream world of Fair Hill, Menlough and beyond.

It was always a summer of freedom and fresh food, home-cured bacon straight from the barrel, spuds and cabbage out of the drill. It was a return to the tribe, a place of endless story-telling, of wondrous superstition and vivid speech, including the odd word of Irish. This was our own Wild West. It even connected oddly to the cowboy films in Bill Egan's cinema back home in Callan. When we dived into the mysterious, pungent holes of the bog after a day of desperately failing to foot turf, we came up gasping, tanned like Comanches. For a while we sported brown faces, at least until that next, inevitable shower of rain.

The West of Ireland has always exerted an uncanny pull upon the Irish consciousness. This pull affected me as a child, as it has affected numerous writers and artists over the years. The journey westward is, above all, a journey of the imagination. Perhaps it is an attempt to recover the possibility of promise, something that has been lost by the Irish and because of its very lostness can be retrieved only through the romantic imagination? When I eventually came to read the rich literature inspired by the West of Ireland, I did so carrying the memories of my own childhood.

For instance, I had made my own journey westward long before I read Joyce's short story 'The Dead'. In the cadenza of Gabriel Conroy's mixed feelings at the end of that story you have the perfect expression of this mystique of the West of Ireland in Irish writing:

> A few light taps upon the pane made him turn to the window. It had begun to snow again. He watched sleepily the flakes, silver and dark, falling obliquely against the lamplight. The time had come for him to set out on his journey westward. Yes, the newspapers were right: snow was general all over Ireland. It was falling on every part of the dark central plain, on the treeless hills, falling softly upon the Bog of Allen and, farther westward, softly falling into the dark mutinous Shannon waves.

In the ending of his story Joyce was returning to a favourite area of his, between wakefulness and sleep, one that he would return to again and again in his writing. It is a place in which sharp edges, most importantly the precipitous one between life and death, are gently dissolved in the flowing rhythm of language. Joyce was drawn to this flow, as he was to the constant tendency in language to evade exact meaning or to indulge in multiple meanings, all that languid avoidance of the regimentation of grammar and the finality of the full stop.

But what is it that made Joyce associate the West of Ireland with dissolving consciousness, with the impressionistic blending of outlines, with romantic love and loss, even death? The story of the Galway boy in 'The Dead', Michael Furey, had a lot to do with it, of course, and behind it the early life of Joyce's wife Nora Barnacle, and her own story of her young man Sonny Bodkin back in Galway, the source of Joyce's fiction. But Joyce the writer is responding here to something else as well: the seductive appeal of the western landscape to many imaginative writers and painters as a place that gives a peculiar fillip to the imagination, most especially to those who remain mere visitors to this region and who know it best through memory.

That drifting movement westward is described by Joyce with the precision of a map-maker. It begins by crossing the River Shannon. Each Shannon bridge was a portal. This, surely, was the true frontier on the island of Ireland and not that other, political partition farther north? The great river is a much more ancient, more rooted line between one kind of experience of Irishness and another. Much Irish writing in the twentieth century has been a negotiation, a mediation, a discourse between these two sides of the Irish experience, the east and the west, the anglicized and the gaelicized.

Language is central to all this, the loss of one language, the adoption of another. The process was slow and was least effective west of the Shannon. Since language was a badge of conquest, this had serious political implications. To the English mind, the West was associated with barbaric customs and general unreliability, a fit dumping ground for undesirables from other parts of the island. This was effectively summed up in the Cromwellian taunting command to the native Irish uprooted and dispossessed by the new settlers, telling them to go 'To Hell or to Connacht!' No wonder the place assumed such an aura for the Irish themselves, particularly those in exile from the island.

Writers have always been drawn to the Irish west as to a lodestar, from Maria Edgeworth to Thackeray to the founders of the Irish Literary Revival, Yeats, Lady Gregory and John Millington Synge. When Yeats sought a mythical figure to embody this attraction, he chose Antaeus. This was the giant wrestler of mythology who drew his strength from physical contact with the soil. Hercules learned this secret and lifted the monstrous wrestler into the air until the strength seeped from him and he could be killed.

Contact with the soil for Yeats, Gregory and Synge was contact with folklore and the remarkable fact that the riches of Gaelic tradition survived not only in the manuscripts of libraries but also in the living oral tradition of the people. The custodian of this tradition was the West of Ireland peasant or fisherman. Yeats's fisherman in 'gray Connemara cloth' is one such figure, an embodiment of this late-Romantic celebration of the man close to nature, untainted by the deadening features of modern metropolitan life.

Synge took this romanticism a stage further. There was a hard, ironical centre to him that penetrated deep below the charm and the delightful speech. Like Beckett, he had an almost monkish reverence for deprivation. In part, it was their reaction to their similar, comfortable, middle-class background on the anglicized east coast. But it also had to do with the discovery of value in a very impoverished area. What gives the characters of Synge authenticity is their dispossession. Out of this material penury pours the golden hoard of language and stories.

In the Ireland of my childhood it was still possible to experience something of that world that so animated Synge. But I knew that I also had to face the life of a small Irish town with its alternative history of conquest and anglicization, its awkward collisions with the modern. While I came to love the older Ireland, I think I was also aware at an early age that I was imaginatively drawn to that more awkward, urban process by which the country was growing into something new. This pull in different directions was part of my childhood and of my growth as a writer. It is little wonder that I became so obsessed with history. It is also little wonder that I grew so preoccupied with the divided self.

As it happened, there were two figures from the Callan area when I was growing up who represented aspects of these alternative Irish traditions. They were to make substantial contributions to Irish culture in their own, very different work, and both examined both sides of the Irish experience. These two were the painter Tony O'Malley, from the town of Callan, and the essayist and activist Hubert Butler, from the nearby village of Bennettsbridge. I knew both of them. They were like two examples, two models of how to engage the world in which I grew up, addressing many of the issues that I was to face myself as a writer.

Tony O'Malley spent thirty years in the art colony of St Ives in Cornwall but returned to his native Callan in 1990 and died there in 2003 at the age of ninety. His father, too, was from the West of Ireland and I remember conversations with Tony about that journey westward, which both he and I took as youngsters from Callan back to the paternal and also, in my case, maternal, home-place. I remember him talking about the different rhythms of life and language to be found west of the River Shannon. O'Malley's sense of release in journeying westward was very much like my own. I also remember his description of our two fathers, who were pals, chatting together, leaning against a wall and extolling the virtues of the West of Ireland of their childhood, two displaced persons on a small island. For Tony they were like two Irish exiles in a South Boston bar talking about home.

Tony was a wise man as well as an artist and knew that nothing is quite as simple as it might appear to be. He said two things about this business of the West of Ireland, with that distinctive chuckle of his buried deep in his beard. One was that he wondered how long this quality of life would last in the western counties. The truth is that it has already disappeared and the West of Ireland is now largely indistinguishable from the rest of the country. Tony's other remark was that, finally, at some essential level, as an artist, it didn't matter where you lived.

When O'Malley looked at the people around him in Callan, he saw a deep, almost silent quality that outsiders could mistake for emptiness. O'Malley, however, with a Zen stillness within himself, was capable of seeing the rooted quality of the people of Callan and the strength behind the silence. He also wrote with a deep historical consciousness about the character of the people. He identified this, most of all, with their use of language and the presence of stone in the Callan landscape:

I think that the Callan character is cool, detached and observant, a few words here and there, with an underlying reticence ... . Their articulate side is still there; they could say what they wanted to say in a very few words without any ornate dressing ... . In a Callan pub, you would get a man talking, he might say a few words ... and then a profound silence descended again. Callan was a feudal town, a walled town, which explains its quality of interiorness.

There is something of this potent silence in O'Malley's own work. When he turned for inspiration as an artist to local material in Callan, he found it in the stone carvings of cemeteries and abbeys like nearby Jerpoint Abbey. He followed the work of the families of stone carvers such as the O'Tunneys and O'Sheas, about whom we know very little beyond the names. All we have is that astonishing carved stone they have left behind them.

O'Malley found this kind of painting extremely difficult because he was putting the effect of incised stone onto canvas with paint brushwork; in other words, he was painting stone. For him, these stonemason families represented links with a more ancient Gaelic, pagan past, going back beyond the anglicized Callan, bringing their wild sketching on stone from that past into a Christian Ireland. In other words, they were like ghosts from the West of Ireland.

Tony loved this confluence of the ancient and the modern and particularly its element of comic surprise. He loved the wry doodling he found in the Kilkenny stonework, which is like the comic drawings of Irish monks in the margins of medieval illuminated manuscripts, a deflation of self-importance and piety.

One of the features of modernism in art has been its attraction to primitive expression on the periphery of the modern, an attraction to the elemental, to the ability of the primitive to reduce everything to an essential, even abstract, image. Like Gauguin in Tahiti or the modernists of the early twentieth century who also turned for inspiration to primitive art, O'Malley was discovering a neo-primitivism for himself in the churchyards around Callan:

In drawing a skull, the O'Tunneys drew a rectangle, two ellipses, an oval vertical and then just a grin. That was simply powerful. Picasso would have been overwhelmed if he had seen them, they were so abstract. Our idea of painting now is exactitude of description, but these fellows had a power over abstract forms. They drew a hammer, it was carved in stone, it was still a stone but it was a hammer ... just a hammer and a nail and a crown of thorns. They understood stone. So too did the O'Shea brothers from Callan, who carved the witty animals on the Kildare Street Club.

But there is another side to O'Malley's painting other than the darkness of Kilkenny stone. This side brims with colour and the swift movement of drawing, a response to everything that is fecund and mobile in life. I like to think that this light, lyrical quality in O'Malley's painting, the profusion of colour in a marine setting, owes as much to the West of Ireland island heritage of his people as it does to the release he experienced when he first went to the Bahamas. It was not unlike the response of Synge to the West of Ireland and his excitement at the discovery of 'a popular imagination that is fiery, magnificent, and tender'.

The most famous Norman name around Callan is Butler. When William the Conqueror conquered England in 1066, one of the Norman knights who came with him from Normandy was one Herveious Walter. The descendants of this Walter were rewarded for their loyalty to the crown with the hereditary title of Butlership (le Boteler), first of England and later of Ireland. This was how the Butlers of Kilkenny and Callan acquired their name.

One of the quaint honours of the Butlership was the right to present the first glass of wine to the king after his coronation. This takes on more significance in an age gripped by fear of poisoning. The Butlers went on to become, firstly, earls, then marquesses, then dukes, of Ormonde with the family seat at Kilkenny Castle, ten miles north of Callan.

James Butler became the first Earl of Ormonde. A younger brother, John, was to become ancestor of the Callan branch of the family. The Butlers were connected by marriage to Marshall who had given Callan its charter. In time and with a spreading that is characteristic of the family's history, they replaced the Marshalls altogether, acquiring not only Kilkenny Castle but the manor of Callan as well.

There were several places around Callan when I was a child that carried strong associations with the Butlers. One was West-court, the nearest thing that Callan had to a 'Big House', located across the river from the town proper. It and its sister house at Kilcash, in nearby County Tipperary, were the principal homes of the Callan Butlers in the eighteenth century.

My interest in Anglo-Irish culture partially came from my interest in the Butlers. In our Christian Brothers School in Callan we were taught that the Protestant Anglo-Irish landlords had ruled the countryside for England up to the foundation of the Irish Free State. In our classroom everything was laid out in straight lines between the oppressor and the oppressed, the oppressor Anglo and Protestant, the oppressed Irish and Catholic. I just had to look around me at the way in which the Butlers had proliferated in Callan and Kilkenny, crossing lines of class and religion, to see that this strict line between the Anglo-Irish and the native Irish was in need of a qualification.

It was clear from the family history of the Butlers that Irish history is a tangle of criss-crossed lines. Colonel John Butler, a nephew of the first Duke of Ormonde, occupied Westcourt in Callan in the early eighteenth century. His nephew Christopher was the Catholic Archbishop of Cashel. Christopher died at Westcourt but is buried at Kilcash. As children, we were once shown a path at Westcourt where the saintly archbishop was reputed to have recited the rosary with residents of the big house. In the native language, Irish, no less.

Kilcash, the sister house of Westcourt, is situated across the county border in County Tipperary. It rests on the slopes of Slievenamon. This was the spot where our picnic outing to climb

Slievenamon began and near where I saw my mother and the clatch of women talking furtively about the story of the burning of the 'witch', poor Bridget Cleary.

Kilcash is now recalled in a haunting lament in the Irish language on the death of Margaret Butler, the lady of the house. The form of the song is a remarkable fusion of two cultures, Irish and English, a Gaelic *caoine* or lament, but written in the nine-teenth century, an imitation of a much older, Gaelic tribute to nobility, an ancient Gaelic form adapted by the Anglo-Irish:

> *What will we do now for timber?*
> *The last of the forest is down.*
> *Nothing more is to be said of Kilcash and its household.*
> *Its bell will never ring again.*

Another Butler, one Piers, gave his name to a Callan castle. There was no trace of it in my childhood but I knew where it stood at the end of Mill Street and I had heard its name, Coortpherish or Pierce's Court. This was the castle later occupied by the Callan garrison during the Cromwellian siege of the town.

These Butlers were the 'hard-riding country gentlemen' of Yeats's phrase. The poet's full name, of course, was William Butler Yeats and he was very proud of his rather tenuous connection to the Butler family on his maternal side. He was to include Butler in his roll-call of ancestors fighting for the House of Orange in the Williamite War of the late seventeenth century:

> *Soldiers that gave, whatever die was cast:*
> *A Butler or an Armstrong that withstood*
> *Beside the brackish waters of the Boyne*
> *James and his Irish when the Dutchman crossed;*

The Butler Society today lists sixty-five different branches of the family across all the continents, including von Buttlars in Germany, Boutlers in France, Butelers in Argentina and Boutlerov in Russia. In my own time the name was shared around Callan and County Kilkenny by carters and carpenters, shopkeepers and nurses, as well as the odd retired colonel, which demonstrated how the family had spread itself in other ways as well.

In my lifetime the most significant Butler from the Callan area was the essayist, intellectual historian, translator and activist in the cause of human rights, Hubert Butler, who died in 1991 at the age of ninety-one. It is true that, growing up, I had only a vague sense of his presence. As a student I had only a bewildered sense of his fierce questioning of the value system of the Catholic Ireland from which I came. I regret that. I might have grown up more quickly if I had attended to what he was writing.

I met Hubert Butler no more than three or four times in casual, if sometimes intense, conversation and I have a couple of letters from him and that was it. He said he admired my novel about Callan, *The Big Chapel.* On one occasion he asked, with that stern, aquiline glare of his, where I had found the inspiration for the character Horace Percy Butler in that book. I hummed and hawed and tried to look into the middle distance, and the question died in the air between us. The truth, of course, was that one of the inspirations for that nineteenth-century, eccentric, abrasive observer in the novel was himself, although the characters were utterly different. I was unable to say this to him but, of course, he must have known it.

Our paths crossed in curious ways. He wrote about Ireland, Europe and America out of journeys he had made. In the early 1960s he travelled through the American South on a Greyhound bus recording the turmoil of the Civil Rights movement. I was there myself teaching at Vanderbilt University in Nashville, Tennessee, two years later where I had my own encounters with the racism Hubert Butler described.

He wrote of the local and the European with equal engagement. He wrote about that witchcraft case, which I had experienced myself, as a child, amongst the skirts of the women and my mother on the slopes of Slievenamon.

Butler also wrote, with first-hand knowledge, of the corruption of Catholicism in post-war *Mitteleuropa*. He wrote about Europe of the dictators. When I hitch-hiked – with great difficulty, it has to be said – around Franco's Spain in the mid-1950s, I hadn't yet read Butler's analyses of rigid fascism. When I smuggled dinars in my socks across the border into Tito's Yugoslavia in 1957 (dinars were dirt cheap in the black market outside the railway station in Trieste), I didn't know Butler's work. I had no idea at the time how Butler's writings could have guided me, making sense of all that senseless tyranny. His essays were to reinterpret post-war Europe in all its impoverishment when I did come to read them later in my life.

Throughout the essays, Butler recorded, sadly, the demise of his own Norman, Anglo-Irish culture. He looked upon this heritage with a wry humour: 'My father belonged to the minor Anglo-Irish gentry and, except for remote kinship of blood, had no link with the two or three noble Butler dynasties which still reigned nearby, and which we were to survive in Kilkenny.' Butler also translated Chekhov. When I eventually came to adapt Chekhov's *The Seagull* to an Anglo-Irish setting for the Royal Court Theatre in London in 1981, I have no doubt that the figure of Hubert Butler stood near me.

Joseph Brodsky described Butler as 'a dishonesty hunter'. He also remarked upon the startling fact that this most cosmopolitan of men, a man at home in the heart of Europe, chose to spend the better part of his life outside a small village near Callan. But this is one of the most precious legacies of Butler: his sense of place, one closely linked to his sense of history.

He was, and remains, an extraordinary presence in my life, a man of the Enlightenment, of a mind addressing the world as it actually is, not as one would wish it to be. He accomplished this with a piercing, angular intelligence and a capacity to see truth through the murk of human stupidity and destructiveness. Above all he revealed to me that history is something that exists in the present tense, entwined in the contemporary narrative, all-pervasive and an essential instrument in understanding the modern. My need to imagine history in historical fiction as one would imagine anything else comes from this sense of history intruding into contemporary life.

Over four hundred years after the town received its Norman charter, Callan was once again crushed by an invader from the neighbouring island, Oliver Cromwell. When I began to assemble notes for this book, I knew that I wanted to include the Cromwellian siege of the town. It had gripped my imagination as a little boy. But how could one do this in a book of memory?

As children, we may not have read the history books yet but we had heard the grim stories of the Cromwellian soldiers passed down from generation to generation in the town. Under our feet there was a stirring of the past. Our games were invaded by something more potent than print; we learned history from the feeling of grass under our bare feet.

At the top of the GAA pitch in the fair green behind our backyard was a grassy hillock, the outline of an old Norman moat. It was a companion of the much larger moat near the bridge over the river at the other end of the town. But the one in the green had long been levelled when the nearby road to Coolagh and Wind Gap was being laid out in the nineteenth century. All that was left was this low outline of the original mound. A place to play on. And so, on Cromwell's moat, as the local people called it, we played at Cromwell with our wooden swords and makeshift helmets of war.

Tradition, as they say, has it that this was the site of the Cromwellian cannon in 1650, trained upon the town walls at the other end of the fair green. As children we were playing in a place of slaughter, although we didn't know it. I cannot begin to describe the power this fact has exerted upon my imagination. I knew I had to imagine what this siege was actually like in all its horror. The odd thing is that, in doing this, I somehow grew closer to the child

I once was, standing on the moat and waving his wooden sword. I am also aware that some great writers have confronted childhood memories with similar, adult perspectives, in effect laying down one kind of recall beside another, the one enhancing the other.

For Wordsworth there was something sublime about the innocence of childhood with its open access to the mysterious 'Presence' in the natural world. But this is not the complete picture for the poet. He has to bring in the perspective of adulthood, looking back upon childhood, informing it with knowledge of the world as it really is. This is how the American critic Carlos Baker illustrates this, the way the poet employs two antiphonal voices in the great 'Immortality Ode': 'Here is the picture of the true innocent, trailing his clouds of glory, clothed with the sun. Yet here beside it is also the voice of experience, neither harsh nor grating though deeply informed with the knowledge of the possibilities of good and evil.'

There is a similar matching of the vision of childhood with its opposite in William Blake's *Songs of Innocence and of Experience*. These opposites do not cancel out one another. They retain their integrity. But they meld in a mysterious unity that rises off the page in a great arch of meaning.

So I have invented two local boys from seventeenth-century Callan, one of whom has bad eyesight. They are the first two from the town to catch sight of an advance party of the English army. We see the horror of war through their eyes. We see what happens to each of them as the siege works its way towards the destruction of the town.

But there is one other layer to this evocation of seventeenth-century Callan that should be included: the documentary record, such as it is, of the siege itself. How does the historian describe the journey of Cromwell towards Callan in 1650?

Cromwell had wintered in Youghal in County Cork on the southern coast at the start of his Irish campaign. When he came out of winter quarters, in January, he split the army in two, taking one section himself in a sweep through counties Cork, Limerick and Tipperary. He sent the second and larger section of the army under a Colonel Reynolds towards Carrick-on-Suir in County Tipperary. From there Reynolds turned towards Callan and it was his cannons that were planted on the moat on the green behind our house on that February day when the town was taken.

Reynolds's behaviour at Callan was merciless, although Cromwell tried to excuse it. Reynolds was, however, known for his decency in his treatment of Charles I before the king's execution. He was the one Commonwealth officer who spent time walking with the stricken monarch before his execution, trying to calm him down, on the bleak Spit of Hurst Castle by the River Solent.

On his march from Youghal, Cromwell eventually arrived in Fethard where he heard of what was happening to Reynolds in nearby Callan. It appears that, by the time he had arrived in Callan, the town had fallen.

Here is Cromwell's own account of what happened in his report to the Parliament back in London after the siege:

> From thence I marched towards Callan; hearing that Colonel Reynolds was there – When I came thither, I found he had fallen upon the enemy's horse, and routed them (being about a hundred) with his forlorn; he took my Lord of Ossory's captain-lieutenant, and another lieutenant of horse; and prisoners one of those who betrayed our garrison of Enniscorthy; whom we hanged. The enemy had possessed three castles in the town; one of them belonging to one Butler, very considerable; the other two had about a hundred or a hundred and twenty men in them, which latter he [Reynolds] attempted; and they, refusing condition seasonably offered, were put all to the sword.

4

THE ARRIVAL OF CROMWELL

A Fictional Interlude

The Lord hath been pleased to make choice of these islands wherein to manifest many great and glorious things.

Seán had bad eyes. Sometimes they ran with a watery discharge but mostly it was like watching everything through a fine mist. His mother told him that his eyes would only get weaker as he grew older and that he would have to make up for this in other ways. This drew a line between him and his mother and he looked away from her to try and find those other ways, as she called them. Despite the bad sight, he was one of the first from the town to spot the Roundheads.

'Lookit!' he cried out to his pal Murty, pointing.

'What?' said Murty, not looking. 'What ya talkin' about?'

Murty was more interested in tying the dead rabbit to the rope around his waist. But then he looked up. Five men on horseback were picking their way down through the famished wintry skeogh bushes and scutch grass of the slopes and ridges of Baunta, with Wind Gap away above in the distance. On the opposite bank of the little river the two boys, shivering, watched the soldiers advance. Everything stood out in that cold, blue, February air.

'Come away, Murty,' Seán whispered, not for the last time on that day of slaughter. His head was spinning, as often happened when he saw something that he couldn't exactly make out. Murty was a bit slow but he meant everything to Seán. For one thing he never mocked his friend's bad sight as other boys in the town did. He would sometimes take a stick to them when they yelled at Seán, 'Crooked eyes! Crooked eyes!' Murty hunted them away then. Everyone in the town except Seán was half-afraid of Murty because you never knew which way he would go. Seán was very proud of not being afraid of this boy, who was as big as a grown man. Both of them were without fathers, although they never talked about this. They were well known around the town as a pair, the small boy with the squint and the tuft of red hair, the big dark one wide as a barrel.

What Seán was watching and only partially seeing was a scouting party of five men. Two troopers were out in front with metal glittering. Grilled helmet bars over the two faces, breast-plates over the buff coats and red tunics. One trooper's coat was sleeveless. As if to compensate, he wore a bright orange sash around his waist. The second trooper was comically fat but not comic to the two boys. He wore a metal bridle gauntlet, a black, shining metal glove from finger to elbow. It was like an extra, monstrous hand and arm. Seán couldn't see these details but he saw the size of the English horses. Could these monsters really be horses? He had never seen the like around Callan.

Seán knew there was no hope of shifting Murty when there was half a chance to watch soldiers. Anything in a uniform attracted Murty's attention. Seán didn't say so out loud but he thought this fascination ridiculous. Immature was a word he thought of, a word that he had found in a book. He stood behind Murty. He was always standing behind Murty's stout back with its tattered shirt and the ring of dirt around the collar. He liked having Murty between him and possible trouble.

'Stay away from that fella,' his mother had said, 'he's no good, so he's not.'

The three sisters had watched this exchange in the kitchen, waiting to see how it would turn out. But Seán wouldn't give in. He wouldn't renege on Murty, come what may. There were times when he felt Murty was rescuing him from the female nest that was home. If he hadn't Murty beside him there was a lot he couldn't do.

At Murty's feet the hob ferret coiled and sprang in its box. Seán hated that ferret with a vengeance. He was secretly afraid of it and he hated his own fear.

'There'll be coin for rabbits, you'll see,' Murty had said in the town earlier as the boys watched the people make ready for the siege, boarding up doors and windows. 'Once they close the gates, they'll eat anything in this town, so they will.' That was how the two had ended up hunting rabbits by the river on the day the English army approached the town.

The ferret threw its lithe, vicious, golden body from side to side in the box, not in terror but in rage at being enclosed, its little red eyes darting this way and that. Murty could hold the snake head of the ferret with one hand, even when it sank its fangs into his wrist. Seán wouldn't touch it unless he had to and then with a quick dart of the hand, quickly withdrawn. Across the box lay the home-made muzzle of wire and canvas for the ferret's head. This was Murty's own invention, used when the boys wanted the ferret to flush out a live rabbit from the burrow. This time, though, they had been hunting to kill. The dead rabbit, with its blackened bloody head and wide swollen eyes, now swung on the rope around Murty's waist.

Seán wiped his eyes. The men came on. Behind the two troopers were the three others in the party. A strange man in black, with a high, steeple hat, and two scruffy assistants to either side. These three were on normal, smaller horses, the man in black on a grey, the two assistants on cobs. They were carrying an array of implements and satchels, outlandish pipes and curious instruments with measuring gauges and rods. Seán knew that these three weren't real soldiers.

The five Roundheads reached the ruined wall of Magner's Mill, the river between them and the two boys. The man in black spoke. For the first time on that day of days the boys heard that new, strange, harsh accent of the English. It would ring through the streets of the town during the days following in the midst of the bloodshed.

At the words, the two assistants jumped off the cobs, instruments toppling. The first trooper surveyed the countryside, lazily. The fat one saw the two boys. He pointed. He barked out something that the boys couldn't understand and pulled a carbine from behind his saddle.

'Murty!' Seán cried out again, but Murty just stood, stock still, his eyes on the two soldiers and the three oddities.

All five men were now looking across at them. Then the man in black gave a shrill order. A wicker ladder was unfolded and placed at the wall of the mill, held steady by an assistant. The man in black climbed the ladder with excessive care, nursing his bones, a long eyeglass under one arm. Up above, he turned the glass on the town.

From the riverbank the town was just visible above the tree-tops. But from his perch all was naked to the eye of the man in black: the town walls, the castles, the great South Gate with its two towers. Perhaps he could even see My Lord of Ossory's horses, wheeling and displaying themselves like coloured peacocks on the fair green before the South Gate?

Much earlier, at first light, before they came hunting rabbits, the two boys had watched the Irish cavalry assemble for manoeuvres before the town walls.

All the gentlemen from the county and beyond were assembled, displaying their finery on horseback. Purple and blues, greens, saffron and reds, each man had his own array of coloured coat and britches, each his own elaborate brocade and stitching across the chest and down the flank, each his embroidered baldric with its sword, each his wide hat with its elaborate, waving feather. Murty knew all about them and explained to Seán that this was the cavalry to take on the men of Cromwell. Seán could only marvel at the colours on display, even though he couldn't pick out faces.

Cloaks were tossed back over the shoulder for easier movement of the arms but also to display the silk linings of matching colours underneath and the wide collars of white linen and lace at the throat. Some sported matching handkerchiefs at the wrist. Many of the gentlemen had body servants in attendance, some more than one, fussing with cloaks and wigs, boots and spurs as if they and their masters were still in chamber and not on the battlefield.

The two boys had stood on the edge of the green with a scattering of country folk, awkward as always near the town, mouths open at this great presentation by the better people. The wall of the town was also thronged with onlookers, mostly women and children, who shouted and clapped their hands from on high, like watchers before a puppet show or a masque.

Lines of racing gentlemen obliged with a practice gallop, sweeping down the green with swords aloft. They ended each charge against nothing by slashing the air with their swords and doffing their hats towards the excited ladies above them on the wall. Then they turned away smartly and galloped back to their first places, to be followed by another mock charge.

'What're they up to?' asked Seán. He could see no point in what they were doing. He could never see the point of armies. Murty looked vacant whenever Seán questioned the subject of armies. For Murty, armies were everything and he told Seán he was going to join up at the first chance.

There was much congratulation among the riders. Every one of them was thrilled. Bugles rang out. Everybody said the town was safe with such stout defenders. Everyone said that the English would never stand such a charge from such mighty valiant horsemen. Everyone said it would cost the invader dearly this day before the walls of Callan. A chilled fear swept through Seán's body and his narrow shoulders shook.

Back on the bank of the little river the man in black issued another order in that harsh tongue and an assistant scribbled instructions into a book. This went on for some minutes while the fat trooper continued to stare across at the two boys, his gun now upright in the crook of his arm.

Then Seán became aware of something new. This often happened to him where he could sense something without seeing it. He had to search before he found what it was this time but by then he was shaking with terror again. The eyeglass had been turned on Murty and himself. He could even see the glint of sunlight from the glass. For some moments the man in black observed the two boys from his stand on the wall.

For the first time Murty shifted slightly, a delicate movement of his big feet, no more. But Seán saw it. He watched the feet and waited, ready to run if Murty ran, his chest tightening. He was waiting for Murty's signal, as had often happened before, when the two were in a tight corner, poaching pheasants in the Westcourt demesne or raiding an orchard out in Tullamaine or Kilbricken.

But Murty's signal never came. It didn't have to. A galloping sound and two dragoons on small fast horses came racing up the riverbank from the direction of Castle Eve. These two wore knitted Monmouth caps pulled down over long, flying hair. Bandoliers of powder boxes swung from their chests and both carried muskets in one hand. When they wheeled in towards the group at the Mill, Seán saw what looked like a golden trumpet on one of their backs.

The boys were quickly forgotten. There were shouts to and fro between the men, with arms pointing towards Castle Eve and the distant highway to Kells and the southwest. All seven men turned their horses and galloped away along the riverbank from where the dragoons had first come.

Now, for the first time in their lives, the two boys heard the sounds of a great army in motion. They then realized where the seven men were headed. They were going to join the rest of the arriving army. The boys could hear the army of the English, the distant sound of a great mass of men and animals in motion, coming from the Kells road. At first a low rumble, the cranking of wheels. Then came the crack and stumble of many horses, the rhythmic thudding of marching feet, the creaking of line after line of carts. A vast murmuring hovered above this thudding and creaking. It sounded like an argument of voices. Only later were they to learn that it was prayer.

When the two boys came racing back to the green from the little river, all had changed from before. The troops of cavalry were still drawn up before the South Gate but now in grim, silent formation. Two wings of horse in rows of three troops, each with a gap between the wings, all facing the arrival of the enemy. The stillness was fearful as they listened to the rolling sound of the moving army coming nearer and nearer out on the Kells road.

By the South Gate the reserve were drawn up with a knot of mounted officers in consultation. One officer flourished an eyeglass. A few marksmen stood on the town wall with fowling pieces and muskets. The women and children were nowhere to be seen. The watching country people, too, had withdrawn to a safe distance, although their heads could be seen peering over ditches.

By the edge of the green was a stand of old trees, which the boys knew well. It stood opposite the moat, the high, grassy hill that dominated the south end of the green. Many a time they had played on the moat. They would hide in the branches of the trees when one of Seán's sisters came calling for them from the town. Seán wondered where she and her two sisters were now. He wondered if they and his mother had left with the others from the lane, fleeing along the road to Kilkenny. He put the thought out of his head before it could make him afraid. Murty was heading towards the trees without a word.

Shouldn't they tell someone what they had seen by the mill? panted Seán. He knew that Murty would never think of something like that. There was a lot that never bothered Murty. Seán sprang at the tree. If there was one thing he had over Murty, it was agility. He ran and climbed like a monkey. He was halfway up the tree before Murty reached it. Murty said nothing, the ferret in a furore in its box and the dead rabbit dangling. He had trouble following Seán with all this baggage, never mind his weight from all that eating. When he got up into the tree, the two saw and heard, but not everything.

The creaking, rumbling noise of the approaching army had suddenly stopped as if a command had been issued from on high. The boys heard the drumbeat that followed but could not see the parley before the East Gate and the Castle of Coortfeerish. This was where Sir Robert Talbot commanded the main garrison of the town. This was where the fate of the town was agreed, although few were to know it then. Talbot was negotiating to save his own skin.

The two boys watched, Seán desperately trying to make out details. They saw runners scurrying from the direction of Coortfeerish towards the cavalry command on the green, once, twice, three times, to tell, it would seem, what was afoot at the other side of town. The officers on horseback by the South Gate debated with heated words at what they heard. Some withdrew into a separate huddle. Some engaged the keepers of the South Gate in shouted exchanges. But nothing changed. The drawn-up troops of horse on the green were unmoving. The officers remained where they were to the rear. The enemy army on the Kells road remained hidden in its great silence.

And, then, without a signal of any kind, the enemy horse appeared, moving onto the green like actors taking their place upon a stage. What Seán saw was a line like a snake, a wavering line undulating across the field. The snake stayed in his head long after he recognized the horsemen.

It was said afterwards that no one had ever seen such a horse formation before, except in the drawings of old books. It was said that it was little wonder that My Lord of Ossory's command was so confused by what confronted them. They had formed in the recognized arrangement of *battalgia* to meet the brunt of their foe. Now here was this formation, like something from a carnival or an old book.

Two by two, in a long column of gigantic horse, the English entered the green at a smart trot. By the sides of the column several officers cantered up and down, issuing short, sharp commands. To one side a preacher sat on horseback with book aloft, competing with the cries of the officers in his continuous, droning invocation to the Almighty: 'We beseech you in the bowels of Christ, remember what God for you and us hath done at Marston Moor, Naseby, Pembroke, Tredah, and upon what grounds!'

But it was the weaponry that most shocked the waiting cavalry. Each Roundhead was carrying an upright pike, its point glittering in the air high above the head of the holder. In this day and age cavalry did not carry pike.

The bemusement of the Ossory horse did not last long. Suddenly the double column of the Roundheads split in two, one line veering to the right, the other to the left. The waiting cavalry watched in fear, some shouting out warnings.

Now there were two snakes in Seán's mind, curling with menace, the columns of Roundheads moving away from their prey, their backs actually turned on the Irish horse, some of whom were now breaking rank in fright, despite yells from their officers. Within minutes the Roundheads reversed and turned in two lines to face the Irish, a scissors about to close. Two or three sharp commands rang out. Then they charged the Ossory horse from opposite sides, pike heads down over the horses' heads in the gallop, like knights of old at a tourney.

The first collision was all the greater because of the speed and distance of the charge. A heap of shrieking horses and screaming men went down on either side of the field under the hooves of the gigantic horses of the English. The troops of Irish cavalry caught up in the middle tried to gallop back towards the South Gate where their officers and men of the reserve sat watching with horror. Others, breaking through the mass of churning men and animals on the ground, were cut to pieces by the Roundheads. There was no escape. The whole formation of the Irish was squeezed into a narrow press of man and animal, shuddering on the ground like a single, floundering beast, legs aloft, in its death throes.

So forceful was the blow that Roundhead almost met Roundhead on opposite sides across the field of slaughter. On their great animals they waded through the roiling sea of upright, shaking legs of the smaller, dying Irish horses, the hats and feathers of men flying like kites in the air. Horse and man alike were targets of the pike. Tendons and necks of the animals were particularly sought out and slashed to the bone. Dazed men with wigs askew or bald pates exposed were gored where they fell to their knees or staggered about dazed, hunted down, impaled into the ground.

At close quarters the Irish took some of the Cromwellians from their horses with pistol and sword, but very few.

Then came an unexpected apparition as if from nowhere. ''Tis a doctor,' Murty whispered in his throat, 'they have 'em in the army.'

Seán saw only shadows. What was he talking about, doctor?

A surgeon, a large man with shaven skull, huge arms bulging from a leather smock, appeared among the English fighters. He was followed by his team of three helpers pulling a two-wheeled cart. When two arms of this contraption were put to the ground in front, the item became a table for the wounded.

In and out of the heaving throng of horses and men this fearless medico led his helpers, oblivious of blows about his head, of sword and pike shearing the air, pointing, and searching out men for treatment.

By narrowing his eyes, Seán eventually picked out the surgeon standing by the cart, implements aloft. The injured English were dragged free by the helpers and put on the wheeled table to the side. There the surgeon, like a bloodied wrestler, set to with his knives and pliers on the dazed body of the injured man, held down by his assistants. Some injured were pushed back afterwards, bandaged, into the fray again after treatment; others were dragged off some distance to recover or die. The surgeon rushed on in search of more victims, with his helpers falling over themselves behind, trying to keep up with his demented search for more damaged bodies to work on. In the busy assault upon bodies, fighter and surgeon appeared to become as one in their quest for victims.

It was a painful assault on Seán's eyes. He had never seen so much happening in such a small space of time. It was like a crushing against his forehead, and his whole head sang with the prickling images. He laughed and Murty looked at him in heavy puzzlement. But Seán didn't know what he was laughing at. His laughter was a dry cackle in his throat, and in his dizziness he thought he might topple from the tree. He looked away from this grotesque comedy to try to recover. Then he saw what was coming next. 'Look,' he cried hysterically, pointing again. Murty paid him no heed. He was drugged by the savagery laid out before him on the green.

What Seán saw, although he could not put a name to it, was the arrival of the Forlorn, the shock troops of the Cromwellians, mad men with red faces and eyes aglint who wore bloodied rags like honoured decorations and would rush to the front when called for, men with the mark of death already on their faces even before engaging in battle.

Four troops of dragoons and two companies of foot of the Forlorn moving smartly. As if anticipating their arrival, the pikemen turned in strict unity as one and left the field with the surgeon and his team trotting behind them. A handful carried wounds and one or two horses were riderless.

The dragoons formed a half-circle, dismounted and made ready their carbines. Some set up musket rests, others just stood ready to fire from the shoulder into what remained of horse and men on the field, the odd animal stirring or trying to rise, one or two men dragging a comrade but going nowhere. The cries of pain on the field were drowned out by a loud moan from the town walls, although no heads were visible above the parapet. Seán put his head in his hands but couldn't rid himself of what was in front of him.

At this point, the Irish officers at the South Gate made the unhappy decision to order a charge of what was left of their force. But the horsemen who galloped forward in a line were impeded by their fallen comrades in front of them on the field so that they had to leap and duck down the green like huntsmen in rough country.

At an order, the dragoons turned their arm pieces from the dying towards these charging horsemen. They held their fire until the horses were almost upon them, then fired with perfect discipline. Over half the horsemen were wiped out and fell, crazed horses running in all directions. What was left of the charge turned and scrambled back from where it had come.

'I have to go,' Seán said to Murty, 'I have to.'

'You're going nowhere, boy,' said Murty grimly. 'Turn your back on it if you must.'

Seán knew he was right. There was no escape. He didn't turn his back. He watched with Murty.

Out on the green the dragoons parted with precision and the Forlorn infantry poured forward in the third assault. These fellows walked into close contact with the piles of dying and dead on the ground. These butchers were ground workers. They worked in darting pairs or groups of three or four, all attention to the job in hand, it requiring a peculiar temper to kill those already dying.

One might raise a dying man by the shoulders while others ran him through with sword or dagger. Some of the dying were decapitated, blood gushing upon the indifferent killers. Pistols were used to dispatch both men and horses with flickers of movement and puffs of smoke. After such a display of horse colliding with horse, these death-dealers looked diminutive, like insects across the hide of a carcass. Their baggy, blood-spattered pants gave them a slightly clownish look, heads down and tails up, as they rooted among the fallen, fishing out the slightest sign of life so that all might be snuffed out.

The Irish officers by the South Gate were now frantically trying to negotiate terms, throwing down their arms and dipping their colours in submission. Surprisingly the English appeared to have lost all interest in them and were waving them away. Go! Go!

But when the Irish started to move off there was a sudden flurry of action from the English. They dragged one Irish officer from his horse. In sharp order a gibbet was produced and the man was hanged before he knew what was happening to him. The rest of the Irish cantered away, leaving their hanging comrade. He was still hanging there on the green for weeks after the fall of the town.

Meanwhile, the English demonstrated their need to cleanse the field. The troopers had put aside their pikes, standing them upright in the turf to one side of the green. In this way they were free to become cleaners of the field that they had just recently devastated. Busy helpers came running from the direction of the hidden army, carrying cables and pushing handcarts. Ropes were tied to dead horses, bodies were thrown onto carts and in a short while much of the mess of the dead had been shifted. A deep groan arose from behind the town walls at what was going on but no one was visible.

The corpses of horses and men were dragged away out into the commons beyond Madd's Ditch. Soon the first of many pyres to be lit around the town in those days of siege flared up with dark, acrid smoke. The heavy smell of burning flesh, of clothes and leather, floated across the town and countryside. In this way the field had been readied once more for the next action to take place.

The main army now rolled into the green. Nothing had prepared the two boys for such a show of might. Murty sat trans-fixed, still gripping the box with its ferret. Seán shook with terror. Although he was terrified at what he saw spreading out in front of him, Seán was equally aware of things right beside him in the tree. He felt a great confusion at such different things happening at the same time. His mind tried to juggle with everything but it couldn't keep up with the details. Beside him, Murty was coiled with atten-tion like a spring about to leap. The ferret was still, not a scratch or a scurry from him in his box. Seán even leaned forward to look, half-hoping the creature might be a goner. But he was alive all right. Seán could see the eyes winking at him out of the dark.

By the town wall Sankey's regiment crossed in perfect order, spick and span, passing by the walls and the South Gate but beyond range, even if there was anyone brave enough to fire at them from the parapet above. Although they were strangers to the place, the soldiers seemed to know exactly where they were going, like men with maps in their heads.

'Will you look at that!' Murty breathed in immense satisfac-tion. 'Did you ever in all your life?'

On the English marched in the direction of Dirtystep and the distant West Gate, hidden around the curve of the high wall. Just under a thousand men. Ten closely marshalled troops, each troop with its pair of drummers, loudly drumming, each with its ensign and flag-carriers, sergeants and corporals to the front and rear.

Out ahead rode the colonel and his officers like gentlemen on horseback taking their pleasure in the open air. The rear was brought up by carriages and wagons with light field pieces and a small troop of dragoons. Although the boys were not to see it happen, this was the first division of the invaders to enter the town by the undefended West Gate.

When this insolent display had passed by, most of the rest of the English army moved much more slowly onto the green, so that the place was soon teeming with horses and men, wagons and carts. At one moment all was chaos, then, very quickly, a pattern appeared and all was order again. It was a mystery to Seán, the whole business – one minute all this confusion, the next minute everything settling into place.

The great assembly of men and animals had divided, the larger portion of the army moving away towards Tinnamona and where the green reached open countryside and the Clonmel Highway beyond. There it began to settle, with the ranks dividing again and again to this side and that, marking out territory. Engineers and their helpers ran hither and thither with tents and cables, poles and shovels as the men settled down. Colonel Reynolds himself and his regimental staff chose their quarters in the middle of this main body. Soon the tents of the command post were rising there, with flags waving above.

Seán had never seen anything like it. He always thought a war would just be fighting and fighting, without stop. But here there had been that first terrible charge of the cavalry and now this strange kind of normality had followed. The crowd of soldiers seemed indifferent to the town, shouting between themselves like men at a street corner or sitting down on the grass like men passing the time away, smoking their pipes. But there were even more startling things to come.

The smaller section of the force had remained closer to the moat, immediately in front of the boys and their tree, leaving a great swathe of open ground between the moat and the South Gate, several hundred yards distant. The purpose of this open space was now revealed in quick order: *If I am necessitated to bend my cannon upon you, you must expect what is usual in such cases.*

Lines of horses, tethered to one another, one behind the other, ten or twelve in the line, came pulling large siege guns, creaking on the high wheels of limber carriages, across the green and heading towards the moat. Two or three riders were spread along each line, spurring the horses on with cries and whips. Men ran alongside, helping with the wheels, turning the spokes with their arms like great hands upon a clock face, to advance the train across the soft grass. Behind this train of artillery walked the solemn gunner crews with their baggage and tackle, their long linstocks and ladles to prime the weapons. Behind them again, and at a distance, came the carts with the painted red signs of warning that they were carrying the dreaded powder and ball.

Although the boys couldn't see it from their perch, a division of the army under Colonel Ireton had been left behind before the Castle of Coortfeerish at the Kells road and its cowed defenders. This meant that the town was now surrounded by three detachments on all sides, south of the big river, the Avonree. The river itself had been deliberately flooded with dams in the weeks before the siege and blocked with great stakes and bulwarks as a northern line of defence. The English ignored it. They wished to make a different demonstration other than swimming.

Men were clambering to the top of the moat. Pulleys were set up and the heavy business started of pulling the guns and equipment up onto the rise. Many a time the two boys had clambered up that slope themselves. They had often played with their own mock guns on that same summit.

Seán felt a new terror, like a cold drench across his body. Part of this terror came from the speed at which everything he had ever known was being changed for ever in front of his eyes. Murty couldn't contain his excitement.

'I'm off!'

'Where to?' whispered Seán.

'Down there! I hafta see this. Up close.'

'Are ye mad?'

'I hafta.'

'You go down there and yer finished, so ye are.'

Even Seán was surprised at his own vehemence. It was as if it wasn't himself talking but someone else, someone he knew and didn't know at the same time. He wondered what in the name of God was happening. Was anything ever to be the same again?

Murty had paused, though. This was another surprise since Murty never paid all that much heed to what was said to him, perhaps especially by Seán. Murty was now watching intently as the men worked at the great guns, a cannon and a demi-cannon with one mean-looking, long-barrelled saker. Wicker gabions were packed with earth by a line of shovellers and were quickly raised to the top of the mound to shield the guns. An ugly squat mortar, fat and wide, with its wide open throat of a barrel turned upwards towards the heavens, was left to one side at the foot of the moat, out of sight of the town.

Before Murty could make up his mind whether to go or stay, there was yet another distraction. This one headed straight towards the clutch of trees where the boys were hidden. It couldn't be more different from what had gone before.

A raggle-taggle of what looked like gypsies and scavengers, a hodgepodge of different carts and wagons, a gallimaufry of outfits, mostly in tatters, came dawdling along, not in files, like the soldiers, but in waves of disorder and noise. There was much bawling and shouting and even laughter from this arse of the army, the baggage train, bringing up the rear of the march but bringing essentials as well. A small troop of bored cavalry seemed to be guarding this horde, though who would bother with them was another question.

At the head was a moving village of artisans, sooty smiths with bare arms, filthy kerchiefs knotted around their heads. Heavy carts carried their smithies, anvils and bellows and the makings of fire. These were accompanied by what turned out to be a crowd of craftsmen, carpenters and metal beaters, mechanicals and stitchers, some with leathern aprons, some wearing old guild caps with faded insignia. Then came the food trains, carts rattling with hanging saucepans and skillets, toppling cauldrons and pots. Cooks and cook-helps, a jollier group, walked alongside, many of them pointing towards the trees where the boys were hidden.

'They've seen us!'

'They couldn't have!'

'They have so!' said Seán. 'Look at them pointing at us.'

He wondered if he had been right to stop Murty from leaving when he did. Maybe they could have escaped at that stage? What if they were trapped in the tree for the duration? But Murty was right. They hadn't been seen at all. What the English were pointing towards was merely the shelter of the trees.

The food train had its share of Irish hangers-on and vagrants, toadies and side-swappers, who had been picked up along the road, hanging around, trying to fit in without being noticed, hoping for the odd scrap of food from the tables. Here, too, were the women of the army. Large-boned women with wild hair who linked arms. Some of them were singing. They seemed to have their own general. A tall woman in a cloak shouted frequent commands and directions at the gigglers and gossips around her. Finally, came the herds of cattle commandeered in the last few miles, rounded up from farms along the march to the town. These were driven by drovers and overseen by a team of animal butchers.

Out on the commons, beyond the ditch, groups of troopers were still tending the dying pyres of the men and animal victims of that first charge. This was where the cattle were driven and gathered in makeshift fencing near an old stone wall. Before the battle for the town commenced, the cattle were systematically slaughtered. Beef for the army. Feeding and killing, killing and feeding, beast and man. The kitchen train moved in under the trees so that the two boys could look down directly on the busy activity below. Like the gunners on the moat, the cooks and their helpers, including the women, began working at great speed. No one got in the way of anyone else.

Sure enough, by the time the first gun hissed and belched, sending its first shot across the clear ground, the cooking fires were lit behind the trees. Trestle tables were set up in lines and old awnings of canvas strung above them like shelters at a fair.

Murty watched the gunners with a knowledgeable air. ''Tis to try and find the range. That's all they're doing,' he explained to Seán.

'How d'ya know that?'

'See them big guns behind there? Them're the ones for to knock walls down, so they are.'

He turned out to be right, as per usual. How did Murty know so much when everyone said he was a thick? Seán felt a twinge of shame at his own helplessness, as he often did when Murty was proved right about something.

The waiting army was watching the gunnery like an audience. It wasn't like any war Seán had ever heard of, this sitting around, waiting and watching. Why weren't they all fighting?

The first shot hit the board of the South Gate, a firm crack of ball on wood. Another groan came from behind the walls but this one lower than before, like a lost call from down a deep well.

But the gunners weren't happy with their results. Their target was elsewhere. Close discussions were going on behind the wicker barrier on the moat. Instruments were produced and the angle of the gun muzzle was measured several times by men wielding rods and quadrants, like a group of alert tailors.

The cooks and their helpers were indifferent to all this drama. They had their own drama, laying out the grub. Slabs of meat were thrown onto grills over the fires. Huge vats of barley gruel and mutton broth were hung on tripods over other fires. Loaves of bread were being chopped on the tables and large rounds of yellow cheese were unrolled from canvas bags. Piles of wrinkled apples were at one end of a table, kegs of beer and tankards at another. The two boys slavered at the sight of this feast and Seán realized that he hadn't eaten anything since daybreak. There was something that wasn't right about his hunger now. No one should be hungry in a place like this. The food was for the troopers and dragoons of that first charge. They came forward from their tending of the cleaning pyres out on the commons. Their horses were tied up and they sauntered along in groups to the tables, laughing, joking together, the first to fight, the first to be fed.

The saker gun on the moat came to life again and the shot rang out once more, clean as a whistle in the air, followed this time by the crack of ball on masonry. Seán saw that they were now aiming at one of the Gate towers. When he turned back, he realized that Murty was on the move. There was no stopping him now.

'What're ya doin'?'

'I'm gettin' some o' that grub.'

'Ya'll be kilt, so ya will!'

'No, I won't.'

'They won't give ya anything.'

'They will so. Haven't I this? A fair swop!' He was holding up the dead rabbit for Seán to see. Then, without a word more, he was shimmying down the branches to the ground.

It was only then that Seán saw there were local country people down there as well, with hands outstretched, begging for food. But Murty had gone straight to the head of the queue, plonking the dead rabbit down upon a table. Everyone was greatly taken by this newly arrived entertainment. The men awaiting their food in the line shouted and laughed and pointed at Murty. He was surrounded by women who poked and pulled at him, at the ferret box and at the dead rabbit. The men shouted encouragement to the women and the women ruffled Murty's head, some of them grabbing the rabbit. It disappeared quickly. One of them gave him bread and cheese and Seán was half-annoyed that Murty had been proven right once again. There was no danger. He decided he'd better get down there fast while the going was good.

When he reached the ground, the sound of the gun from the moat was deafening, which gave him pause. But the women saw him now and he was dragged forward to join Murty at the table. Murty winked at him, his cheeks full of bread. There was a barrage of strange language from the men and women and slaps and shoves from those around him, so that for a moment Seán was dizzy again, dizzy with the strange talk, the smell of food and the boom of artillery. Then a shadow crossed above his head. That was all. A shadow.

A single horseman. The troopers in their lines before the tables guffawed at this apparition. Seán looked up. The figure seemed fixed to the saddle, away up high above him on this gigantic horse, a bedraggled knight still carrying his upright pike long after battle had ended. In spite of all the laughter about him, Seán was afraid. He had never seen such tiredness on a face as on that beneath the helmet: gaunt cheeks, sunken holes for eyes and stretched yellow skin.

The men guffawed even more but the ravished face looked down at Seán. Seán wanted to talk to Murty behind him but he couldn't take his eyes off this face. This wasn't a man on the horse. This was a boy. Not much older than Murty or himself but changed by this mask of exhaustion far beyond any normal sleep. Lank, fair hair fell down on either side of the helmet and there was the beginnings of a beard on the long narrow jaws and chin, just a squiggle of fair hair.

Suddenly the right hand holding the pike swivelled and moved with great speed over Seán's shoulder sending the point into Murty's chest behind him. Seán heard the crack and splintering of bone and a deep gasp from behind his back. He turned to look. A twist and the pike was free again, Murty falling splat on his face, blood everywhere. The men guffawed even more loudly at this turn of events and there were cries from the women, egging on the rider to further action.

Murty was face down on the ground and Seán was somewhere he had never been before, some new and terrible place with no name to it. He had seen death many times in the town but never that of someone so close to him. He looked at the horseman, trying to understand, but the horseboy looked back at him with this nothingness on his face.

Another lightning twist of the right hand and Murty's back was pierced this time, the blood spurting upwards in two or three threads. With a final flourish the pikeman lifted the box with the ferret in it and crashed it to the ground. The animal leaped free and the men cheered, pointing out what had happened to one another. The women yelped and lifted their skirts as the ferret darted this way and that between the tables. Then it was gone.

Seán looked at the killer. I'm going to die next, he thought. He felt nothing, just this shell where his body should be. He had a desperate need to cry but there were no tears. He also needed someone to say something to him, anyone, anything. He tried to think of his mother and sisters but there was nothing in his head. They might as well have been among the dead.

The soldiers had already turned their backs on what had happened. It was over and done with. The grim horseboy, alone, stared at him as if to say, See! This is what I can do, whenever I want to! Seán tried to walk towards Murty but someone pushed him away. The last thing he saw was women dragging away Murty's body between tables. His one thought then was that there might be no one left in the town for him to tell what had happened to Murty. He thought again of his mother and what she had said about his finding other ways to go in his life. Is this what she meant? That nothing would ever be the same again?

The English seemed to have forgotten all about him, while the killer on the horse had disappeared. Seán didn't run. He staggered away, heading off in the direction that he and Murty had come from when they first saw the Roundheads by the little river that morning, which now seemed such a long, long time ago. The guns were booming behind him in concert but he kept going in a state of broken confusion. Nothing could frighten him ever again in the old way. Nothing.

All that day and most of the night following he stumbled and sank through a dark netherworld of briars and bushes around Prologue and Tinnamona, circling and circling beyond the encampment of the foreign soldiers and their sentries. Still he came dangerously close, now and then, to the odd squatting soldier beneath the trees. As often happened, the gathering darkness gave relief to his eyes and he thought at times that he could see better with the daylight gone.

He had to get back into the town to see what had happened to his mother and the girls. But how? He just had to. He was terrified of the guns. They roared and spat and sizzled into the evening. Sometimes he met knots of townspeople crouching down in hedges and ditches. They called out questions to him but he couldn't answer. 'Murty is dead,' he said to one man who looked at him as if he were mad.

As the darkness fell, the mortar started its explosions, flaring, hot balls arcing into the sky, clearing the town walls in fire and sparks and then crashing beyond. Screams came from the town and great fires shot up into the night sky as the mortar found its mark on thatch and timber. The people around him in the ditches crossed themselves and said it was the end of the world.

Somewhere in the darkness he passed a line of white-faced children holding hands with bowed heads, walking slowly along in silence. They were minded by two women, one at the front of the line, one at the rear. A small army of ghosts out of the darkness, disappearing again as if Seán didn't exist.

He slept sitting up in an old outhouse in Prologue near where he had often come looking for hazel nuts at Bealtaine with Murty. He could feel nothing. He tried saying to himself, He's dead! He's dead! But he felt nothing. He wondered if he was to be frozen inside like this for the rest of his life.

At first light he was awakened by the roars and weapons of the first assault of the English on the breach of the South Gate but he kept well away from it. When he reached the West Gate, all was quiet except for the distant sound of the fighting at the other end of town. To his astonishment, here was a line of farmers' carts laden with produce: milk, potatoes, turnips and trussed fowl, all lined up, waiting to enter the town as if it were a market day. The farmers chatted and smoked their pipes as if the fighting above on the green was in a different town entirely. His mind wobbled again at this strange mixture of normality and terror.

The sound of battle soon died down. When it was all over, the English soldiers let them through the West Gate, paying no attention to Seán sitting on the back of an ass and cart. Inside, the ruined town was like a body cut open from neck to crotch.

The roof of Skerry's Castle poured smoke into the sky. Piles of bodies everywhere; many he recognized despite their mutilations. Men, women and children, some with vicious white blisters on faces and arms, burned by the boiling water poured down into the castle from the roof by the English. To one side a sullen group of women prisoners. He saw the long red hair of the wife of Captain Geoghegan but there was no sign of the man himself. It was said, a farmer whispered to him, that Geoghegan and the wife had killed ten English in Skerry's Castle before it was taken from under them.

'Don't go up the town!' the farmers warned him in whispers. 'No man or boy is safe from the English! They'll send you away on the boats.'

But that was where he had to go to see if his own home was still standing. He was driven. He skirted the burning houses of West Street through backyards and garden plots until he reached The Cross. The great wooden crucifix, which had stood in place there with its lantern since ancient times it was said, was now shattered in large fragments. In its place were seven gibbets with hanging priests and friars, but no townspeople were visible. If they were watching this display they were doing so in hiding, like Seán. There were soldiers everywhere, guarding the four streets that met at The Cross from north, south, east and west, and lines of prisoners were being marched down North Street towards the river.

Seán ducked, running through the garden of the Inn. From behind a cracked fence he looked out onto South Street and St Mary's Church across the way. The soldiers there were lounging by the side of the street. The big medico with his assistants from the battle on the green were busy again tending the wounded at a makeshift station near the Tholsel. Seán thought of Murty again and he began to weep for the first time, snuffling into his sleeve.

St Mary's was being ransacked. Old men and a few women of the town stood watching the desecration but the soldiers paid them no heed. Vestments and chalices, gold patens and other items had been piled up on a table outside the church. There, several clerks were busily recording the findings into large books.

Seán went up the lane by the side of South Street until he came behind Collopy's shop. The door into the yard behind the shop was open and he was about to go in when a *psst psst* sound came from over his head. Mrs Collopy was signalling frantically to him. He could see the narrow face of the widow framed by a broken window high above him in the shed. The goitre in her neck wobbled. Beside her was her son Josie the simpleton, with his usual rictus of a grin. Seán almost laughed at the sight of the two of them. They looked like a Punch and Judy. But then he heard the harsh whisper of the woman:

'Where d'ya think yer goin', young fella? Is it for a stroll? Have ya taken leave of yer senses, young lad? Don't ya know that death is aswagger up and down the street out there? Every tenth man in the rank and file is knocked on the head be the English. The rest is sent down to Waterford Quay to be shipped to the Barbadoes. Is that what ya want, young lad? Well, bechrist they won't get me son Josie, so they won't, over me dead body, the curse of hell on the whole pack of them; they're all the same in uniform, English and Irish alike.'

Josie giggled at his own name.

'They've put us outta our houses. Go live in the shed, they said, like common animals. They've taken every house on South Street for themselves. They write their own names into the book for every house that's standing. There's no place for ya to go, young fella. The lanes is all burnt out.'

On she went like a something wound up. Seán staggered away. He passed the big gates of Regan's timber yards and looked out on

South Street. There was a new commotion down at The Cross. The English soldiers and a few townspeople were gathered, watching in absolute silence. From East Street came the surrendered garrison of the king's army from Coortfeerish Castle. The portly knight Sir Robert Talbot and his officers rode at the head. All their weapons had been surrendered and they turned into North Street and the river and the long march ahead of them before they would reach the Royalist lines farther north towards Kilkenny.

Seán saw his chance. He scooted across the street and into the laneways of the town. The widow Collopy was right. All down the lanes houses were smouldering in ruins, a few old people searching and sifting in the ashes. He knew what to expect now.

Not a sign of his mother and sisters. He arrived at his own doorway and stepped across the threshold into his burned-out home. He was shocked at how small it now looked without a roof and loft. He felt he could reach out and touch the far wall of where the kitchen used to be, without moving. How did they all fit in here, his mother, himself and the three girls? There were piles of broken delph among the ashes on the floor. The table had only partially burned; two legs and half the table top stood propped up in the middle of the floor like something on crutches. *I've been touched by these foreigners,* he told himself. *They've marked me with their weapons. I'm like Murty now.*

He hunkered down outside the doorway in the bitterly cold air and a strange feeling descended upon him. He couldn't understand it but he knew he would never be the same again from this day out. A great determination had seized him. He would rebuild the house, he told himself, for his mother and sisters, and never once did he doubt that they would all be together again. Home, he said quietly to himself. Home. It was such a soft word. But what was coursing through his body was anything but soft. It was hard and heavy, like iron.

He thought of Murty now as someone he had known a long time ago and in another life, even though they had set out only yesterday with the ferret and the ferret muzzle and caught a rabbit near the little river and were the first people of the town to see the Roundheads. *If he were to meet me now, Murty, he wouldn't know me. He'd walk past me as if I were a stranger.* These thoughts gave him great satisfaction.

He got to his feet and left, walking through the town as if he owned the place. The English soon latched onto him and put him to work. They were glad to find a local who could read and write. He gave them names and he watched in fascination as the scribes wrote down details of the town in their big books. Why did they have to write everything down, he wondered, when they have now conquered the place?

Two nights later a scattering of bullied townspeople gathered on the town wall near the battered South Gate. They watched the arrival of the second English army from Fethard. The whole countryside seemed to be occupied by the English, now settling down for the night. Lines of fires and tents ran off into the darkness. Male voices were singing in the distance but mostly it was the sound of men and horses shifting and shuffling and settling around the fires.

One of the two towers of the South Gate was now no more than a pile of rubble and the battered gate itself hung open as if about to collapse. Directly below the people on the wall and before the broken gate was a great black tent. It was far bigger than anything else in the fields. Its flap was raised and a golden light came from within. In front of the tent were the colonels of the two armies, standing in stillness beside their horses, no one speaking, looking off towards Coortfeerish Castle. Dark, gnarled, leathery men, the killers of the English king, each with his own small group of sergeants and attendants.

At first, when he joined the people on the wall and looked out, Seán couldn't make out any details. Everything was just a blur, with winking fire after fire spread out into the darkness. Shouts came from the direction of Coortfeerish Castle, shouts thrown from man to man like the passing of a ball in flight. A new stiff-ening took hold of the officers below and all eyes were now turned in the one direction. Then, suddenly, Seán could see. Just like that. It was like a flooding of light into his head. The vague shapes became solid and the forms of human bodies became clear. He was aware of lines of torches marking out a passageway alongside the wall.

A cavalcade of horsemen approached on this passageway and Seán suddenly became aware of colours, black and white but also crimson, green and blue. Soldiers along the way rose to their feet, some doffing their hats as the horsemen trotted past them. When the detachment came nearer, Seán saw that it was an escort of a mounted man in the middle, someone special. He was over-whelmed by this miraculous display of sight. He saw the horsemen reach the great black tent and dismount. He saw the watching officers go rigid with attention.

With intense excitement, Seán saw that the man in the middle was small and slight. He was wearing a shiny black breastplate with white lace at the neck but no helmet. The long white face beneath the flowing long hair to the shoulders seemed to reflect the light pouring from the tent. When the man, finally, stood upon the ground, attendants removed his breastplate and in his long-sleeved white shirt the figure looked even slighter than before, almost helpless. But before he could examine this scene any further, the man was quickly bundled into a cloak and swept into the tent. The officers followed, clumsy and awkward, men not used to repose or the indoors. The commander of the army, My Lord Lieutenant Oliver Cromwell, had arrived in Callan:

> I do not think God hath blest this army for the sake of any one man, nor has His Presence been with it upon any such ground; but that presence and blessing that God hath afforded this army, it hath been of His own good pleasure and to serve His own turn.

5

MY MOTHER AND MY FATHER

Sunday was special in our house. It started on Saturday night and I remember the big tin washing-bath with its two handles (the same one used for washing clothes) being filled with scorching hot water in front of the blazing kitchen stove. We three naked boys were scrubbed clean in an elaborate dance of female decorum involving towels held by my mother and older sister. The sister, as I recall, paid particular and painful attention to the insides of our ears with the help of a soapy facecloth. Apple-red, shining skin and small muscles. We were altar boys at mass in the church, which probably explains the rigorous assault upon the dirt.

Everyone, in Sunday suits, put their best foot forward going to church. My father brushed his good sergeant's uniform and polished his black boots. Each garda was issued with a tin of polish and a curious metal fork with which to polish the silver buttons, each with its stamp of the Irish harp. This metal fork was a flat, brass-coloured plate with a long slit up the middle. Each button slid into this fork until you had four or five buttons in a row with the cloth underneath protected by this metal surface from the lively polishing.

The Roman Catholic Church surely lost the plot when it abandoned the strict sanctity of the sanctuary in churches. Beyond the communion rail and its golden gates was this place of mystery: the sanctuary with its altars. In the Big Chapel in Callan the three altars rose triumphantly towards the roof in a display of marble, gilt and embossed cloth. Females were excluded from the sanctuary, although I remember the nuns dressing the altars with flowers on special feast days. Otherwise it was the domain of the priest and his altar boys. There the priest acted as intermediary between the people and their divinity.

The mass was a piece of consummate, highly effective theatre based upon control and fear. Only the consecrated hands of the priest could touch the host. As altar boys, we were scared by the awful consequences of touching the blessed instruments, the chalice and ciborium. Any accidental spilling of wine or the host led to an elaborate blessing of the affected ground.

Dressed in our surplices and soutanes, we altar boys were allowed to play a small part in this mystery. We carried the paten to the communion rail, holding it under the chin of each recipient of communion. Mouths agape, tongues protruding and eyes shut in devotion, our neighbours lined up outside the sanctuary to receive the communion while kneeling at the communion rail. It was a curious moment of intimacy with them on Sundays that sometimes caused giggles.

One other figure had access to the sanctuary. This was the male sacristan, an ambiguous dogsbody around the church, wearing an old priest's cassock over his regular clothes. He seems to have been chosen for the job because of his oddity. He didn't seem to have the casual, carefree attitude of other men; indeed, he was like a half-priest, with some of that rigid, clerical self-possession of the real priests. Once a sacristan, he was marked for life.

On one occasion during my childhood a sacristan actually died in the church during the night. He must have been locking up when he fell beside one of the large racks of penny candles. They found him in a pool of blood where he had fallen against the large metal candelabrum, having cut himself on its sharp points. When we came in to serve mass, there was much commotion. The body had been removed but the blood was still on the floor.

After mass and before the Sunday dinner an odd ritual took place most weeks in our house. It haunted me throughout my childhood – another of those adult activities that confused and bothered me because I felt I could never understand it. To this day I still do not know fully what it meant.

Mr Connolly was a middle-aged bachelor and the Barracks Orderly in my father's police station. In other words, he spent most of his life behind a desk filling up forms, reports and ledgers, not in uniform like the other guards but in a prim suit, shirt, collar and tie. For many years he arrived into our kitchen every Sunday morning in his neat gabardine coat, carrying his felt hat in one hand and his walking stick in the other. He was a neat, bald, dapper man with a pale sensitive face and thin lips, who talked in a precise Cork accent, saying only what he needed to say. On his way to us, he stopped off at Mrs Moore's shop opposite the barracks and bought a bag of mixed sweets, liquorice allsorts, maybe, hardboiled chokers or Peggy's Leg. These were distributed to us children, although Mr Connolly permitted himself one or two sweets as well, savouring them through his precise speech. He called my mother May. Very few people called her May.

Mr Connolly seldom sat down in our kitchen. Instead, he would stand with his back against the kitchen dresser conveying the latest gossip of the town to my mother in that economic voice of his. Finally, when she had finished whatever she was doing in the kitchen, we all set off for the Sunday walk. We must have presented a sight, a parody of a family taking the air, a man and woman walking behind three tumbling boys and some of the girls out front, playing games that were instantly invented and instantly abandoned, then, off again, to discover some other distraction farther down the road.

What did these walks mean to my mother? Like many pale, red-haired women she looked frail, but this concealed a bony stubbornness that would rise up unexpectedly. She often hinted at the possibility of a life beyond the one she was living and this expressed itself most clearly in the fierce ambition that she had for her five sons, but, strangely, not for her five daughters. She loved gentility. The walk must have been a reprieve from the rough and tumble of the rest of the week, in the company of someone of unusual good manners who treated her as someone special and did so in the courtly language of the loyal clerk. Was he in love with her? I doubt it very much. Whatever these episodes meant, they lacked definition and this, perhaps, was why they frightened me so as a child.

I know what the walk meant to my father, the handsome, tough garda sergeant. He never lost an opportunity to mock Mr Connolly. Mr Connolly was not a 'real' man. He was a 'sissy'. My father used the Irish word *oinseach*, which means a female fool. The taunt would have been withering to a middle-aged man, had he heard it. It was withering to the ten-year-old boy who did hear it. I knew the weight of that word well because my father some-times hurtled it at me when, with my glasses toppling down my nose, I failed to carry out some order he had given me in the way that he had demanded. Indeed, I never had his respect as a child and it was not until I became an academic and a writer in my early twenties that he looked upon me differently. Then our roles were reversed and I found myself much later, an agnostic, reassuring him, the believer, as he moved towards death.

On that Sunday walk we went out the Coolagh Road, past the gate of the fair green with its Cromwell's moat inside, past the pond of frogspawn in Jim Lyons's field with its carpet of slime where we disturbed the frogs and made them go plop into the green, watery mess. We went past the little river where I placed that encounter with the Cromwellian soldiers, turning left into Kilbricken and down to the back end of the town and a new housing estate.

This area had a rough reputation in my childhood and was known locally as the Burma Road, another echo of the war. Back into the town again at that point and up past Egan's garage and the town hall where the concerts and visiting travelling players performed and where I had my first experience of theatre. Then up Green Street to Green View Terrace and home.

This walk was known among the town walkers as the circle. There was something appropriate about the fact that our walk with Mr Connolly didn't have a destination. It merely brought our mother and ourselves back to where we had started out.

On the walk I sometimes stopped, breaking from the game we were playing to look back, confused and anxious at what I saw through my glasses on the road behind. My mother and Mr Connolly walked slowly together, their heads bent, engrossed in conversation. I trembled at the sight. What did all this mean? Why was my father not here? What could they be talking about with such close attention, my mother and Mr Connolly?

My mother was born in 1897 and my father in 1893. They were teenagers together in the small village of Caltra in east Galway in the West of Ireland. She was nineteen and he twenty-three years old in 1916, when Dublin erupted with the Easter Rebellion and Ireland began its War of Independence.

My generation is the last one to have experienced that period of revolution and civil war, not as history but through memory. I don't mean that we can remember the period, because that would be impossible. But some of us experienced it through the memories of our parents and the stories they told us as children.

As young nationalists they joined Sinn Féin and the Gaelic League in their village, under the guidance of the local priest. Sinn Féin was a radical independence movement linked to the

IRA, while the Gaelic League promoted Irish culture and the revival of the Irish language. In 1917 a unit of the IRA was formed in the area and my father became its officer. At the same time my mother joined Cumann na mBan, the women's ancillary group of the IRA, members of which gave back-up help to the armed volunteers. Both were touched by the violent campaign that followed.

My father was the leader of an IRA unit, which attacked a convoy of the Royal Irish Constabulary, the Crown police force, in July 1920, in which two police officers were seriously injured. There followed a period of further attacks and reprisals in the area by the notorious assault units of the so-called Black and Tans. In one such assault on the village of Caltra, my mother's family pub was invaded by the Black and Tans. The family story told how her own mother, my grandmother, Mrs Devine, stood her ground in black widow's weeds and silver grey hair behind the counter while the drunken military shot the bottles on the shelves over her head. The stern old lady I remember from my childhood would have been well capable of such defiance. My mother inherited this dogged determination and, like her own mother, this was remarkable given the fact that they both seemed physically frail to me as a child.

When martial law was declared in the Caltra area in November 1920 my father was rounded up in the general sweep of the countryside and was placed in different detention centres in County Galway. In early May 1921 he and five others were tried before a military court for the shooting of the two policemen. The prosecution depended upon the evidence of an IRA man who had changed sides and given evidence against his old comrades. My father in later years expressed compassion for this man who, he said, had been tortured to the point of mental breakdown. He also said later that the British military officers of the court were both 'fair and efficient'. He and his comrades were convicted and sentenced to penal servitude for life.

The odd thing is that later that same month, my parents were married in the old Catholic Pro-Cathedral of Galway city. Was he allowed out of prison to be married? Certainly, after the wedding, he was back in Galway Jail again and wasn't released until January 1922 as part of the general amnesty following the signing of the Treaty between the British and the leaders of the newly formed Irish Free State government.

While my father was still in prison, another incident took place that nearly caused his death. Although the Treaty between the British and the Irish had already been signed, he was still a prisoner when, in November 1921, six months after his wedding, he was one of the ring-leaders in a violent attempt to burn down Galway Jail from the inside. This was odd: surely the prisoners must have known that they would soon be released under the Treaty? Perhaps it was a last display of defiance against the British authorities. According to my father, the fire was a protest against the maltreatment of a fellow prisoner, Diarmuid Crowley, who was not being given the medical attention he needed. Crowley was a barrister and a judge in the underground judicial system devised by Sinn Féin. As such, he would have been a prime target of the British.

Six revolvers were smuggled into the prison and warders were overpowered as they attempted to open the cells for the daily routine. Five wings of the prison were set ablaze. The military forces, regular units, and both Black and Tans and auxiliaries moved in to surround the prison. Inside, the prisoners sang rebel songs and a battle for control of the prison followed.

The local newspaper, the *Connacht Tribune*, carried an exciting report of the incident: *Dramatic Protest. Political prisoners set fire to Galway Jail. How a captured warder gave the alarm. Ten prisoners and some police injured.* My father was named in the newspaper as among the injured and was listed as 'Thomas Kilroy, camp commandant'. In the press account he was given bravura treatment, like a character out of a play by John Millington Synge:

> Kilroy, who is suffering a life sentence on a charge arising out of the Caltra ambush, got two severe baton blows on the head, and is alleged to have been kicked in the stomach. He

was almost unconscious when taken to the hospital but after his wounds had been attended to he rose up in the bed and declared, 'We got beaten to save the life of Diarmuid Crowley, but we would have suffered death had it been necessary to release him.'

Years later, as a policeman, my father collapsed on a street in Callan with a strangulated hernia and was rushed to surgery. He always claimed that this condition was part of the legacy of the beating he had received in Galway Jail.

Reading through the complete Galway newspaper of the day conveys the surreal atmosphere of the revolutionary period and the lack of clear lines in the narrative, the kind of confusion that attends revolution everywhere. In the newspaper, reports of relentless ambushes and killings of police and military throughout the countryside are placed side by side with the results of games from the local golf links. Masked men drag out victims from their homes on a nightly basis and shoot them while the well-named local theatres, the Empire and the Victoria, continue to do brisk business in comedies and farces. A 'buy Irish' campaign sits uneasily on the page near reports of the more lethal activity of Irish nationalism. Most unnervingly of all, perhaps, Éamon de Valera, the republican leader, is received at the local university in Galway as the new Chancellor of the National University of Ireland in the very same week as the fire in the jail. At the same time as his formal reception by the university, his own rebel soldiers were struggling for their lives in the prison, yards away across the road from the campus.

This was the confused and highly personalized version of the foundation of the Irish state we grew up with as children. My mother spoke less about it than my father, although, despite his record as a gunman, she was always the more radical republican of the two.

Nearly thirty years later, in 1948, I had my first sight of de Valera, then the taoiseach (prime minister) of the Irish state. At the same time I had an early experience of my mother's republicanism. I was thirteen years old.

It was during the general election campaign of that year, a winter campaign with some of the most severe weather of my childhood, when de Valera came and spoke in Callan. The story in Callan was that he had been met outside the town on the Kilkenny Road and put on a white horse with a green cloak around his shoulders. In this imitation of the triumphal parade of an ancient Gaelic chieftain, de Valera made his entrance to the meeting place in the town centre. This happened to be beneath the same lettering on the town hall wall that was covered, as I have described earlier, during World War II. Whether the lettering was still covered or not in 1948, I cannot remember. A stone staircase ran up the outside wall to a doorway high above (as it still does today) and it was from this doorway that de Valera addressed the excited crowd below him on Green Street.

I was in that crowd. I believe my father ensured that some of us children were brought out that night so that we might experience the speech, his way of educating his children in politics. Like many people of their generation, our parents loved oratory and, particularly after a drink or two, my father would quote extracts to us children from some of the great speeches he had heard.

What was the appeal of de Valera to the Irish? A thin, gawky, gaunt figure, he had little obvious appeal in his person. More than that, the voice was a deadly monotone, with a slightly high pitch, and there was little ornamentation or even elevation in his use of language. Yet I can still remember the tension in that crowd on that miserably cold night. Not for the last time in my life I was made to wonder at the power of performance and the way in which it can sometimes create effects that seem beyond nature itself. A performance begins and what was a nondescript figure suddenly becomes transformed in electrifying fashion before our eyes. This was de Valera in action.

Back home, after the meeting, there was a family row.

The most memorable description of how Irish politics disrupts the domestic scene is Joyce's Christmas dinner in *A Portrait of the*

Artist as a Young Man. It, in turn, is based upon Joyce's memory of his own childhood in the fine house in the seaside resort of Bray, south of Dublin, where the Joyce family at the time still enjoyed middle-class comforts. Later, his feckless father would bring the family down to penury. But in the house in Bray there were still servants and silver serving dishes, a genteel lady governess (Dante or Mrs Riordan in the novel) for the children. Indeed, three distinct outsiders who had little to do with one another were at the dinner table, two of whom were Dante and her antagonist, Mr Casey. Like many spendthrift individuals, Joyce's father was the personification of hospitality itself. The Joyce family, mother, father and young James, become the Dedalus parents and young Stephen in the novel. This mixture of family and others was torn apart over the Christmas dinner in a row about the toxic mix of religion and politics and the fate of Charles Stewart Parnell, the great nationalist leader of the Irish people in the nineteenth century, who had become involved with a married woman.

We had a version of the same row, but on a much smaller scale, in our kitchen, over de Valera, my father in one corner and my mother, white-faced and barely controlled, in another. He poured scorn on de Valera, his lip curling in derision. In spite of bringing us to hear Dev speak at the meeting, he now called him the great destroyer of peace in Ireland, the man responsible, above all others, for the Civil War. Didn't he stay at home and send others to London to negotiate the Treaty? And then he rejected the agreement that was made, turning the Irish against one another in mortal combat!

She chanted a different story. Mr de Valera stood up to the English! Mr de Valera wouldn't give in! He wouldn't settle for less than the republic! Mr de Valera wouldn't accept the partition of the country then and he doesn't accept it now, either! Didn't Mr de Valera give Churchill his answer on the wireless after the war? Wasn't the whole world lost in admiration of Mr de Valera and it was only his own who rejected him?

I don't remember how the argument ended but de Valera lost the general election.

What is of interest about the incident, apart from the fact that it involved our parents and that we children were intended as an audience to it, was what it said about Irish nationalism. Down the years the Irish nationalist cause became notorious because of its splits. Each attempted settlement with the British was calculated to cause a split on the Irish side, hiving off a minority determined to continue the fight for a purer, more idealistic goal. The same is true even today with the splinter, dissident IRA groups refusing to compromise and still fighting for the cause.

The story of my parents was the story of the new state struggling to exist after the trauma of civil war. My father took the Treaty side in the Civil War under the influence of Michael Collins and his young Minister for Justice, Kevin O'Higgins. All the evidence is that my mother's sympathies were with the other, extreme republican one. Towards the end of his life, as he became ill with cancer, my father wrote a memoir and I have taken some details from it here.

After his release from Galway Jail in 1922, he had been approached personally by the two men, Michael Staines and Joe Ring, whom Collins had picked to help establish and lead the new, unarmed, Irish police force. They asked him to join and to use his influence to bring old comrades from the IRA with him into the new force. He said that at first he laughed at the idea, as someone who had recently been sentenced to life imprisonment for shooting at two policemen. But eventually he was persuaded and left for Dublin with twenty others from the Galway area.

That night they were given their first test of allegiance in a Dublin hotel. Members of the IRA who were against the Treaty came to their rooms. In a mixture of threats and persuasion, their old comrades tried to get them to go home. However, they stayed and were some of the first new police recruits.

When he was moved with the first couple of thousand garda recruits to the old British military barracks in Kildare, my mother joined him. I don't know what she felt about the new political situation but I do remember her telling us as children about the beautiful married quarters in the camp that were lavishly laid out for their former occupants, British army officers. Coming from the village of Caltra and the small cramped houses there, this would have been her first introduction to something like luxury.

The big issue in the new police force, apart from the fact that the country was moving rapidly towards civil war, was the question of the Royal Irish Constabulary. Members of the old RIC were being drafted into the new police force. Some of these RIC men had shown sympathy for the Irish nationalist cause during the War of Independence and, accordingly, were acceptable to the new recruits from the IRA. But others were offered by the British to help train the new force and set up its structures. It is clear that Collins welcomed this offer of professional help, as he accepted artillery from the British later on to fight the Civil War. But this imposition of old enemies, often at senior rank, was deeply resented by former IRA men who a short time before had been engaged in an armed struggle against them and, in my father's case, actually shooting them.

One of the first things he did in the new garda camp in Kildare, hardly in keeping with his recent oath of allegiance to the state, was to join a secret committee of former IRA men to monitor proceedings in the interest of the IRA. This secret committee became an important influence on the following so-called Kildare Mutiny. A mutinous protest took place among the former IRA volunteers against the promotion of ex-RIC men to senior positions in the new force.

So serious was this mutiny that it almost led to the first shots being fired in the Civil War. My father was in the group of former IRA men who took guns from the camp armoury one night. Armed, they approached the RIC officers who were involved and threatened to shoot them if they didn't leave the camp at once. They left, along with other senior officers. It looked at one point as if the main body of recruits would now join the growing rebellion against the Treaty and the new government. This did not happen. The mutiny actually failed. The senior officers were restored to office and the rebels were obliged to accept in their ranks the presence of some, at least, of the RIC men. This deal was achieved largely through the power and persuasion of Michael Collins and Kevin O'Higgins. Their persuasion had an immense effect upon my father.

In his cups (although he was never a drinking man and a little alcohol went a long way) he would quote vigorously later in life in our kitchen in Callan from two speeches of this period, one by Collins and the other by O'Higgins.

The situation in Kildare had become so dangerous that Collins missed an important meeting in London and came down from Dublin to address the rebellious police recruits in the camp. His speech to them, like the later speech of O'Higgins, was about police duty, the rule of law and the fundamentals of democracy. Its impact upon my father marked his final passage from young gunman to unarmed police officer. He spoke of the way Collins made the distinction between my father and his fellow recruits and members of the old RIC. They would be the first Irish policemen, he told them (unlike the RIC) who would enjoy the support of the people: 'You will start off with the goodwill of the people ... You will be their guardians, not their oppressors, your authority will be derived from the people, not from their enemies ...'

These words of Collins were recited by my father in our kitchen to us children while my mother made the odd sceptical remark from the sidelines. I think what really impressed my father was how, in a remarkably short period of time, Collins had moved from being a ruthless gunman to becoming a constitutional politician. The other speech he recalled was by Kevin O'Higgins. It came later during the early years of the new state.

As Minister for Justice in the new government, O'Higgins was responsible for the board of inquiry set up to investigate the

Kildare Mutiny, and my father gave evidence before it. He told the members of the board, including O'Higgins, that he found it difficult to accept even those RIC men who had shown allegiance to the nationalist cause. In his words to the board, being under the command of ex-RIC men was 'very hard on ordinary men to understand'.

But the speech of O'Higgins, which he remembered so vividly, came years later, in 1927. The Civil War was over by then but the new state still had immense difficulties and found itself unable to pay its police force. My father was chosen as a delegate from County Kilkenny to attend a protest meeting in Dublin against the pay cuts. This meeting was addressed by O'Higgins, still Minister for Justice. His words, once again, persuaded my father and the garda rank and file to put allegiance to the state and the rule of law above personal considerations. These were the words of O'Higgins, which rang out in our kitchen, delivered in good voice by my father: 'You must realize that party will follow party in the ebb and flow of the political tide. You must serve with the same imperturbable discipline any executive that may from time to time be in power ...'

Collins was assassinated in an ambush in County Cork. Within months of his speech, O'Higgins was shot dead on a Dublin street as he walked to church. I think the deaths of both men, and how they died, increased my father's belief in the law and this, in turn, influenced his sons in later life, two of whom became respected lawyers. I am not sure, however, that the same could be said about my mother, and while I have always been fascinated by law and authority, I think I derived my rebelliousness from her.

As a young married couple without children, my mother and father arrived to his first posting in Callan, County Kilkenny, in late October 1922. In the ten months of that year Ireland was to pass through enough history to fill decades. It had signed a Treaty with London, ending the rebellion against the British Crown Forces and bringing to an end the British control of southern Ireland. It

had succeeded in having an election, which ratified these arrangements. It had a new provisional government, which eventually
became secure. There was some success in setting up governing
structures in a country that was also moving rapidly towards civil
war. A new national army came into being, built around those IRA
volunteers who remained loyal to the new state and, of course,
there was the establishment of the new police force. The IRA had
split on the issue of the Treaty. When my father arrived at his new
station, with eight or nine fellow officers, the Civil War was at its
height between anti-Treaty and pro-Treaty forces.

He was to describe Callan at the time as like a frontier town
of the Wild West. For instance, within ten days of the arrival of
the new policemen in the town, the police station was attacked by
masked men and an attempt was made to burn it down. Perhaps,
too, his sense of a frontier atmosphere was partly due to the fact
that, as sergeant, he was issued with a long-barrelled Webley
revolver and twelve rounds of ammunition. This was, technically,
for the shooting of wild dogs, but there is little doubt that it also
reflected the dangerous times. The gun and bullets were stored
in a bedroom drawer during our childhood. I can still remember
its cold, metallic heft and that I could hardly lift it. I can still see
the squat bullets.

Halfway up the narrow staircase my mother had created a
small shrine on a windowsill, a statue of the blessed Virgin Mary.
In front of the statue was a bowl of holy water from the French
grotto in Lourdes. You were expected to bless yourself periodically as you went up or down the stairs.

That gun and those bullets formed another shrine in the
drawer, a dark, dangerous shrine to another creed. When no
one was watching, a small boy made his way upstairs and into the
bedroom. He slid open the drawer so that it didn't squeak. With
difficulty, he lifted the heavy weapon with both hands, trembling
with a confusion of feelings, some of them terrifying. He pointed
the gun as he had seen it done so many times in so many cowboy

films down in Bill Egan's cinema on Green Street, going Bang! Bang! Bang! My mother eventually insisted that my father get rid of the gun and ammunition. He did.

Callan was frontier territory in another sense. It was near the border of counties Kilkenny and Tipperary and the lively competition over hurling matches later in my life was of a more lethal kind during the Civil War. The Callan area itself was of mixed allegiance with both pro- and anti-Treaty families prominent in the community, but Tipperary was one of the principal centres of armed resistance to the Treaty. The leader of the anti-Treaty forces, Liam Lynch, was to make his last stand there in the Knockmealdown Mountains, not far from Callan. Two other incidents involving nearby Tipperary brought the Civil War painfully into the lives of my parents.

In November 1922 the first garda shot dead in the history of the new state was a young man called Harry Phelan. He was from my father's barracks in Callan. Phelan and two other guards had asked for permission to go to the nearby Tipperary village of Mullinahone to buy a hurling ball. My father agreed, provided that they did not wear their garda uniforms. The three were in a pub after their mission when three anti-Treaty IRA men rushed in, one pointing a gun. My father always claimed that he had information that the gun was faulty and that it went off accidentally, killing Phelan. The gunman, a local man called Coady, was smuggled out of the country and was killed shortly afterwards in a New York traffic accident.

The other incident was even more typical of the period. The Civil War had by now reverted to guerrilla attacks by anti-Treaty units of the IRA under Liam Lynch, the so-called Irregulars, on different representatives of the new state, including its police. The Irregulars were led by individuals who had become extremely skilful guerrilla fighters during their campaign against the British. While there was a command structure in place under Lynch, in practice the Irregulars operated as independent, local units.

Everything depended upon the ingenuity of the local commanders. The two most famous of these in Tipperary were Dan Breen and Dinny Lacey.

A month after the killing of the policeman, Callan was taken by the combined units of Breen and Lacey. The daring attack involved three Kilkenny towns in all. In each town the local garrison of the National Army surrendered without a fight and many of the soldiers changed sides, joining the men from Tipperary. It was seen to be so serious a setback for the Irish government that it caused disquiet in London and reached the pages of *The Times*.

My father gave two accounts of what happened in Callan, one written and one in the form of repeated stories to us children, and anyone else who would listen, in our family home. I am following the oral version, partly because of its dramatic flair and partly because it reflects the frontier atmosphere, giving the story a *High Noon*-type moment.

Lacey and Breen entered the town from the Clonmel Road and the direction of Mullinahone where the young policeman had been shot. The two guerrilla leaders were contrasting types. Lacey was thin, ascetic, cold, intellectual-looking and had an extraordinary reputation as a ruthless fighter. Breen was heavy, jocular, swarthy, with bushy black hair and a quick grin. Both of them wore officer uniforms of the IRA.

The Free State troops occupied the old workhouse at the edge of the town and, with the arrival of the Irregulars, the commanding officers immediately surrendered. Those who didn't change sides on the spot were disarmed, marched down the main street of the town and lined up at The Cross. By now the townspeople had crept out of their houses and formed an audience for this demonstration of power and humiliation. Outposts in the town manned by other Free State troops were also taken over and the captured men were given the same treatment. Then it was the turn of the gardaí. They were also lined up on the street before the watching townspeople.

My father was at home with his wife reading the newspaper when armed men banged on the door. He was taken to The Cross and lined up with his fellow police officers. Lacey addressed them, telling them that the anti-Treaty forces had taken over much of the country and that the Irish Free State was finished. He said they could now join the republican fight or face the consequences. Then he walked from policeman to policeman and asked the same question of each of them: 'Name and rank?' For some reason the question was immediately understood and decoded by each man who answered by giving his name and his rank in the IRA in the late War of Independence against the British. Fortunately, each one had such a record. Lacey said, simply, 'Dismiss, men!' The policemen walked away, free.

If there had been any hesitation, if some had been in the RIC, for instance, my father was convinced that Lacey would have shot them. He also told how Breen took him to one side and spent some time trying to persuade him to take off the police uniform and rejoin his own comrades in the fight for the republic. He declined and talked about his oath of allegiance to serve the people in an unarmed, non-sectarian police force, echoing the speech of Collins and anticipating that of O'Higgins.

I don't know where my mother was during all this but I can imagine her accosting the Irregulars, pouring out her respectable record of republicanism to them and demanding the immediate release of her husband. I can also imagine her terror.

Lacey was shot dead early the following year in his native Tipperary in an ambush by Free State troops. His death was one of the events that helped to bring the Civil War to an end. Breen was captured alive, later becoming a constitutional politician and writing a well-known book with the indicative title *My Fight for Irish Freedom.* It was said he could never pass through a metal detector because of the bullets still in his body. Back on that day in Callan, Lacey was thirty-two years old, Breen twenty-eight and my father was twenty-nine. Like most wars, this was a war of the young.

One of the facts that emerged from the memories of my parents in Callan through the 1920s and 1930s was how precarious the new state was, economically, in terms of security, and in the struggle to create unity among its factions. The division of the Civil War and the brutality of both sides were to overshadow those decades and, indeed, to make normal politics very difficult even into my own early life. In those decades there were frequent outbursts of violence. Elections, in particular, put a great strain on the young police force.

Callan was typical of all this and it affected the domestic life of my parents. The place had eleven town commissioners, who were responsible for local government and the giving of public housing. Six of them were anti-Treaty and five were supporters of the government. In their first years in the town my parents had rented a small house from a local businessman, Mr Proctor, who, like many others in business, had a clear interest in supporting the police.

Another, larger house became vacant on Green View Terrace in 1925 and with some uncertainty my father applied for the tenancy. He thought he would have little chance of getting it, given the majority of anti-government representatives among the town commissioners. He got the house. Two of the anti-Treaty side on the town commissioners voted for him because of his old IRA record, an echo of the incident with Lacey and Breen on the street of the town during the Civil War, where membership of the old IRA came to matter more than contemporary politics.

Nine of the ten of us children were born in that house on Green View Terrace, including myself. There was an eleventh child who died in childbirth. His name was Anthony and I clearly remember the small white coffin on the table of the front sitting room, the room that was reserved for special events.

This was the house with its narrow backyard and the fair green behind it where we lived in our imaginations and learned how to hurl. The house had, as I have suggested, a slight aura of gentility to it, particularly in contrast to many houses in the town. This tone was preserved by my mother with a touch here and a touch there of decoration, despite the constant threat of no money. My father was to turn out to be a compulsive gambler.

Her gentility was a brake upon his risk-taking character but he also liked her small, stylish touches. Both of them were proud of our front room (the 'good' room) with its mahogany drop-leaf dining table and pristine suite of furniture, its rose-flowered wallpaper and upright piano, its precious photographs and pictures. The room was off-bounds for most of our lives ('Keep out of the good room!'), though the family gathered there on special occasions such as Christmas. This was the room in which special visitors were received, particularly priests.

Was my mother responsible for the fact that throughout much of our childhood we had a live-in help called Nellie? It seems an incongruous arrangement now, looking back at that small house and the modest income of a police sergeant. Nellie would have had to sleep with the other girls in the girls' room. She was a stout, dark-haired girl, in from the country. She left one black day after yet another row with my father. I remember the three of us small boys running, crying, after her, up the road as she set off, stricken, on her long walk home.

Such small attempted touches of a genteel life belonged to my early childhood. Things seemed to become progressively more difficult as we grew older. At one point early on, for instance, over consecutive summers we went with our mother to a rented house in the County Waterford seaside resort of Tramore. Our next-door neighbour in Callan, a returned Yank called Hensie Gavin, had a large Ford hackney car, which he rented out for excursions, weddings and funerals. We drove in style and in incredible excitement with Hensie at the wheel. I can still remember the faintly sinister, slimy tang of the ocean even before we topped the rise over the great beach of Tramore. Any car trip was also an ordeal for me as I constantly suffered from motion sickness. Our father remained behind in Callan.

My mother was a reader and something of a dreamer, while he cherished facts. We were all commanded to silence while he listened to the tea-time news from Radio Éireann on the wireless. She, on the other hand, was passionate about catching the Sunday night radio play. It was my first engagement with drama and long before I saw proper acting on a stage. Radio Éireann developed a fine school of radio playwrights and an exceptional repertory company of actors who displayed remarkable skills through the medium of the voice. My mother talked during the week about the characters in the play of the previous Sunday night as if they were familiar friends and neighbours. I had found my love of fiction.

They were both of a generation who left schooling after the national school at about the age of thirteen or fourteen. Born at another time or in another place, they would have gone to secondary and third-level education. He would certainly have made a fine, if raffish, lawyer and she could have had a successful career in any of two or three professions. Instead, they poured this energy into the education of their children, determined, no matter what it cost, to get them up the ladder at least above their own level of achievement.

The most surprising thing about my father's life is that he was never promoted in the police force. It is clear that he had leadership qualities. In the very early days he was put in charge of recruitment during the foundation of the force. He also took a leadership role at several early stages of his career in the force. I think the first explanation is that the routine of the work bored him. He detested what he called red-tape or bureaucracy. It is noticeable in his own accounts of events how often he was at home in his own house, reading the paper, when something calling for urgent attention happened back at the police station or on the street. When the first opportunity of an early retirement scheme came in 1952, he took it and left the force. He was not yet sixty years of age.

While in the force he manufactured a kind of alternative life for himself in ventures that were both consoling and risky. One was a large vegetable garden, which he rented on Chapel Lane off Green Street and where he used his agricultural background to good effect in feeding his family with superb vegetables. He spent days at work in that garden from spring sowing into summer and autumn. I can see the figure in the hat and old civilian clothes bent over the immaculate beds of onions, beetroot and lettuces. I can still see the skilful laying out of the autumnal storage pit for potatoes and root crops made with great, traditional craft. The muddied vegetables were in their grave with a delicate surrounding of straw protection. A final clay roofing of the pit was beautifully shaped, like an ancient barrow or tumulus out of an old epic, a triumph in the use of natural materials to keep at bay the decay of nature. We were fed through the winter from that pit.

He rounded us up on beautiful sunny summer days for compulsory weeding around the vegetables while what we really wanted to do was to run off with our old towels and togs to swim in the King's River. His temper was fierce when he was frustrated and tired and he could not understand how we couldn't see the value of the garden and what he was doing for our welfare.

By far the most serious alternative lifestyle he created for himself was with gambling and greyhounds. Because they were small farmers' sons and because of the economy of the country, many gardaí had vegetable gardens on the side. There was also at least one other senior policeman in my father's area who kept greyhounds and went to race meetings. This was serious in that policemen were not allowed to own greyhounds and gambling would have been severely forbidden by the police authorities. The trick was to find a friend, in my father's case a local farmer called Paddy Power, in whose name the dogs were registered. My father's dogs were housed and trained on this man's farm outside Callan.

In the early 1930s my father had several victories at the racetrack, including the Irish Oaks and a victory at Wembley in

London. He and his senior officer made the trip to London and he always claimed that it was this success that set him on the path of gambling. It is difficult to tell at this stage if the gambling had anything to do with his non-promotion, whether or not it created a black mark against his name in the record. After all, the chief superintendent of his division, a gambler like my father and an owner of greyhounds, was with him in London at that race meeting.

His gambling most certainly had an effect upon his domestic life and I remember scenes of anguish and rows when my mother discovered that the latest pay packet had been frittered away at the bookies'. I remember one occasion when, as a small boy I carried a note from my mother to a neighbour looking for the loan of a ten shilling note ('until the end of the week'). The old Irish ten shilling note was beautifully designed and I carried the orange-coloured treasure back to my mother, at least half-triumphantly.

I hated those greyhounds. Partly because, like the weeding in the garden, we were dragooned from our play for duty as 'walkers' of the dogs, taking them for long walks on the leash. I've always thought since then that greyhounds are a particularly repulsive breed of animal, overbred to the point of canine neurosis, sneaky animals capable of sudden attack. Although they were always muzzled on the leash, I never trusted them. I could hardly believe that they were animals similar to our beloved mongrel terrier, Patch.

One of the features of the greyhounds which did delight me, however, was the sound of the names which they were given for the racetrack. His most successful animal was called Killader who, alas, died of pneumonia. But there were others with names like Kerry Brave and Cutlet's Finance. I think part of what intrigued me about these names was the mystery of where on earth he found such names.

What kind of addiction is gambling? Is it simply a desperate attempt to escape the present, intolerable reality? My father regularly bought tickets for the Irish Hospital Sweepstakes, for instance, and would tell us children with absolute conviction each time that he was going to win and transform our lives for ever, while our mother tut-tutted in disbelief. Or is there a form of self-destruction behind each wager? Is the prospect of success or failure of equal strength in the mind of the gambler as he makes his bet? Or has he already passed into fantasy?

Besides the hardship caused to his household, the betting clearly had a deep grip upon my father. There is something touching about his description of it in his written memoir, although his version of it may have been embroidered somewhat:

> After the Wembley affair I unfortunately got into a terrible craze for betting and from then until shortly before my retirement I was considered to be a very heavy gambler. Although I sold numerous dogs, some at the highest prices then prevailing, I lost all or nearly all the money I received from such sales through betting. I learned, to my cost, the unhappiness that excessive betting brings.

Of course, his lack of promotion may have had another, simpler explanation: my father didn't want to leave Callan. The life that he lived there was very agreeable. He enjoyed good relationships, particularly among the farming community. The police work was undemanding. He liked his home on Green View Terrace and the routine of lengthy card games at night with his pals into the small hours of the morning, down the town. He simply put other things ahead of advancement as a police officer.

He once told us children a story about how he actually had resisted a transfer in the 1930s by engaging the support of the local parish priest. His chief superintendent wanted him to move and said he would be a fool not to because it would lead to promotion. At my father's request, the priest organized an appeal in the town against the transfer and this appeal ultimately reached the desk of the Commissioner of the Garda Síochana, General Eoin O'Duffy. The transfer was cancelled. My father in late life was very proud of the fact that he spent his entire service in the one station and he always claimed that this was some kind of record in the history of the force since gardaí were transferred, on a regular basis, from station to station to avoid too close an identification with any one place or community.

He was still glad to take the opportunity of early retirement when it came. He had been dabbling in cattle-dealing and he now used his lump-sum payment on retirement to adopt this new career on a full-time basis. He became a buyer of cattle for a local meat factory. He rented small farm holdings near the town and bought and sold cattle and sheep. Once more we three younger boys were signed up as unpaid labourers. I have a memory of walking unruly cattle at dawn the ten miles from Callan to the fair in Kilkenny, accompanied by much roaring and cursing on all and sundry in the half-darkness.

My father also effected a reversal of farming practice, which proved profitable for a while. He would buy a lorryload of sheep in his home place in Galway. The Kilkenny countryside did not have sheep. This was strictly rich cattle and tillage country. Not only did he sell the sheep to bemused farmers around Callan, he showed the farmers how to take care of the sheep, giving them instructions in cutting out foot-rot, as well as other arcane skills of the shepherd. He would then use the same lorry to bring back a bull from the prized Kilkenny stock and show the Galway farmers how they might improve the puny stock of their milch cows with the aid of Kilkenny bulls.

Besides the determination to see their children through the educational system, my parents conducted an informal educational process at home. It was a question of establishing certain values they shared. Some of these had to do with their own origins in the West of Ireland, the kind of Ireland they came out of, a consciousness of the past, of tradition and of family. The other source of values was derived from the teaching of the Roman Catholic Church. It was simply a fact of life that their children abided by the strict law of the church.

Our summer holidays in the West of Ireland must have been a relief for our mother, just to get children out of the house for a few weeks. For my father, it was also a mission to make sure that we took in something of the tradition that lay like a potent human line in the history of our families. So we learned something of the hardship of peasant Ireland in the nineteenth century and of the infamy of local Galway landlords like Lord Clonbrock.

One story must stand for several. When I was about thirteen or fourteen my father took me to a ruined cottage in the village of Killasolan in County Galway. This was where he and his four brothers and three sisters were raised before the family moved to a better holding in nearby Caltra. The family made the move through the financial help of emigrant relatives in the United States.

My father showed me the single field, which made up the total holding of his family in Killasolan. All that was left of the dwelling were the outline stone walls, about a foot or two high, of the cottage. He told me to walk the overgrown length and breadth of that cottage, from one ruined wall to the other and asked me to think of what it must have been like to raise a family of ten in a space like that.

Behind her strict religious practice my mother displayed the same humane concern for people. It is true she was a daily visitant to the chapel but I feel sure this, too, was a respite from the drudgery at home and the chance to drop in on her friend Mrs Jennings near the church. Again, a single story must stand for her broad understanding of human behaviour.

Some time in my teens an incident took place in the town. An older man had assaulted a boy, anally, with a garage air pump. I was outraged and disgusted and vented my righteousness before my mother at home. She stopped me in my tracks by saying, 'It wasn't at all like what you think it was.' She said 'that poor man' wasn't bad like that, that 'it looked far worse than it really was'. I was silent for a long time after this extraordinary capacity on her part to accept human behaviour, which many of her background would have dismissed with disgust.

Sometimes the West of Ireland of their background invaded their home in Callan like a great Atlantic wind. My father, as a policeman, enjoyed a particular respect among the tinkers, many of whom came from west of the Shannon. This was before the days of political correctness when members of the travelling community were still named for their ancient craft of tinkering, the making and repairing of tin cans, saucepans and other containers.

Whenever a fight broke out in the town between the tinkers or between the tinkers and the locals, he was sent for by the other gardaí. He would set out with his blackthorn stick and bring the trouble to a quick stop. He would also, much to my mother's disapproval, entertain the tinkers in our kitchen. He ignored her complaints and called upon her to produce leaking saucepans for repair. He seemed to know all the tinkers by name and to understand the criss-crossed lines of their family relationships, making enquiries about absent members of the families, Wards or MacDonaghs.

There is one particular memory that is so bizarre that I sometimes think it must be an invention on my part. Two wild-haired men with brazen, drunken faces stand before my father in the kitchen, each with crowding supporters of filthy men, women and children who filled the kitchen behind them. My mother must have fled. The noise was deafening. This was matchmaking between two tribes, although we children didn't understand this at the time. My father was the adjudicator. He sat at his usual place at the head of the kitchen table and laid down the law to the tinkers. There was much wild-eyed, raging argument, much slapping of palms and spitting on the floor. It ended with an extraordinary symbolic moment. Two pieces of metal bar were produced along with a soldering iron. A deal was struck. The match was made (although I can't remember the young couple). The two bars were soldered together with roars of approval and a scattering of sparks all round. Then they all departed like a receding western Irish Atlantic tide after a storm, leaving the kitchen floor in need of the mop.

In his encounters with the tinkers and his risk-taking at the bookmakers, my father had gone off into a region beyond the safety of everyday life, leaving my mother behind him. In this way she became the person of reality and he the dreamer, their usual roles reversed. His was a place far beyond the role of a policeman and I have often wondered at the degree of frustration this pull of anarchy must have created in his life. But they also came together many times as a couple. Never more so than when they broke away from the rigidities of religion and Catholic puritanism. This leads me to my final two anecdotes about them and their responses to my own activities.

At the age of thirteen or fourteen I arrived home from boarding school, St Kieran's College in Kilkenny, and informed my mother that I wanted to become a Franciscan monk. The aspiration, of course, had little to do with religious fervour. It possibly came from stories about St Francis and his communication with the birds. Pictures of the saint and his mastery of bird life were commonplace in our school and I loved the magic of the story, the human command of nature, the notion of a man who could commune with the birds. Or, perhaps, it was little more than a personal fascination with the Franciscan costume or habit, the plain brown full-length robe, which seemed extraordinarily attractive to me in its simplicity and its suggestion of heroic self-denial.

My mother said little to this but summoned me to the kitchen to meet with both my parents, a kind of joint interview that they carried out periodically when a child had to be advised or chastised. He sat at the top of the kitchen table below the wireless with the newspaper spread out before him and she sat away to one side, present but slightly physically apart. Even then, her presence was potent. She may have been to one side but her part in the proceedings was never in doubt.

I was questioned by my father in an unusually gentle tone. There was no sign of the usual figure of authority that he displayed around the house, laying down the law on this, that or the other.

Remarks were made by both of them about the splendid order of Franciscans. They were a fine body of men and no mistake. They were surprised to learn that I had been researching the Franciscan novitiate somewhere in the Irish midlands and that I had its address written down on a scrap of paper in my pocket. I held this out to them and they looked at it, then looked at one another. Both of them agreed that it was a noble aspiration on my part. Both of them were equally adamant that I should put the notion out of my mind at once and go on and study for my examinations and enjoy my hurling. I never suffered from such a delusion again.

My first professional stage production was at the Olympia Theatre as part of the Dublin Theatre Festival in 1968. The play, *The Death and Resurrection of Mr Roche*, was shocking to many people because of its portrayal on stage of an assault upon a gay man by a group of drunken men in a Dublin flat. The one question that preoccupied my two older brothers was: What was to be done about our parents, who were due to travel to see the play at the end of the week? How could they be put off? They had to be blocked from going near the theatre!

In the end there was little need for such anxiety. My parents saw the play. My mother told me she was 'very sorry' for the character in the play who had had his disturbing, physical encounter with the gay man. My father assured me that he had experienced far more terrifying incidents than this one during his days in the guards. Indeed, he offered to give me some of these stories if I wanted to use them in plays in the future. When the play was a success, they were clearly very pleased.

The truth is that, like many of their generation, they escaped the worst features of Catholic puritanism, which were visited instead upon their own children. My brothers and sisters were the ones who were shocked by my play. Maybe the rootedness of my parents in that peasant culture of the West of Ireland allowed them to see human life in all its strange variety, to accept the whole range of human behaviour without worrying about what was normal or abnormal? No doctrinal teaching could restrict such knowledge of nature in all its incredibly diverse fullness.

When he became ill with cancer in his final years, my father suffered terribly. There was at least one occasion when I found myself at his bedside trying to give him some comfort. He screamed that no God could allow such pain. I have little doubt that he was conscious of talking to the one child of his who had lost religion. But I was unable to say to him that I thought all religion was a human invention to keep at bay the brutal fact of death and that, like all human inventions, it was subject to error and corruption. Nor could I talk to him about surrender to death as a return to the rich compost of nature, back to where we came from, although, given his prowess as a gardener, this idea of death as compost might have appealed to him.

Instead, I found myself, an agnostic, babbling out some half-baked idea of immortality, some dream from poetry, which I knew could be of little consolation against that degree of pain. I was not there when he died but I was relieved to hear that he had died in peace with prayers and with members of his family around him while he looked, in silence, from one to the other in turn, as each one recited a decade of the rosary around his death bed.

Even before his death, my mother had already retreated into a silence, with closed eyes, sitting in a chair, in which she spent her last years, a form of death-in-life. When we visited her in the convent where she spent her final days, she never opened her eyes but every so often she would say something, which made it clear that she had been following all the conversations in the room. She had closed a door on the world but, given her immense curiosity about human behaviour, she was still listening.

When the family and friends gathered in the Dublin cancer hospice at our father's funeral, she was also there, sitting in the chair, her eyes still shut. As they were about to close the coffin on him, she screamed out, her eyes now open: 'Let me go to him!

Let me go to him, will you?' There was a silence. No one knew what to do. She went to him, with some difficulty and some help, and standing by the open coffin, she bent and kissed him.

6

HAIR-OIL HURLERS
AND THE PRIESTS

On the Callan Road leading out of Kilkenny city and behind a long high wall sits the faintly absurd pile of St Kieran's College. Its front is a line of buildings with carved balconies and entrance steps in neo-Gothic riot, two wings separated by the thrusting, dominant building of the college chapel at the centre. To the right-hand side of the chapel was the secondary school where my four brothers and I were educated as boarders, although the place was only ten miles from our home town. In those days any journey beyond that of the pony and trap was an adventure. You had to take Tom Nolan's bus to get from Callan to Kilkenny. To the left-hand side of the chapel stood the ecclesiastical college where young men were prepared for the priesthood.

The move to St Kieran's from a small town like Callan may have had its upheaval but it also had its amusing side. Keogh's bakery in Callan produced a particular kind of white bread with a distinguishing crust formed by rolling the dough. This crust had a wonderful flavour, particularly when fresh from the oven, and was much prized by the local people. For some reason the loaf was known as a 'rustic'.

When we members of the Callan contingent arrived on our first day in St Kieran's we were given an entrance examination in basic literacy and numeracy. Part of the English test was a vocabulary question where we had to define a list of words. This test was the brainchild of Father Clohessy, a noted grammarian in the school. One of the words was 'rustic', Father Clohessy having a particular fondness for the language of the past. Much to the general hilarity of everyone but the priest, one of our Callan crowd wrote down 'a sort of a loaf' as his definition of the word.

Behind the extravagant exterior of St Kieran's lay the new confidence of the Catholic Church in Ireland following the Catholic Relief Act of 1782 and the Catholic Emancipation Bill of 1829. The motto of the school, from the Song of Solomon of the Latin Vulgate, *Hiems transit*, 'Winter has passed', says it all. The Catholic Church had reached its springtime by the early nineteenth century after the severe persecution of the previous centuries, which included the dreaded Penal Laws that effectively destroyed the rights of Catholics in Ireland. Its children could at last be educated in a proper fashion, according to the church, that is, under strict ecclesiastical control. Although, mind you, as we shivered with our chilblained fingers and toes through the dark winters of the early 1950s in the study hall and dormitories of St Kieran's, we often wondered about the accuracy of that school motto. Winter seemed to last for at least half of the school year.

St Kieran's was a typical diocesan college of the Diocese of Ossory: in other words, an important part of its function was the education of priests. We were on the other side of the college among lay pupils taking the state public examinations, the Intermediate and the Leaving Certificates. There were day boys as well from Kilkenny and its environs who were much in demand for ferrying forbidden messages to the world outside and smuggling in bars of chocolate and other treats from Kilkenny shops. But mostly the school was made up of boarders.

In my day it was a packed college with over a hundred ecclesiastics and over four hundred lay boys. I suppose the aim of the lay school was to give education to the sons of believers, but the structure of the school must have been based upon the hope that many of the lay boys would go on to study for the priesthood. Indeed, many did, if not in St Kieran's itself, then in one of the many other seminaries throughout the country.

There was another connection between the ecclesiastical side and the lay side during my time. Ecclesiastical students were prefects over the lay boys and, for this reason, were not particularly popular among us. As in any enclosed male institution, there was much emphasis on physical exercise, the idea being that hundreds of teenage boys locked up together should be tired out as often as possible to prevent outbreaks of hooliganism. Apart from hurling and handball, we were expected to take endless exercise when not in the classroom, walking in groups around the many pathways within the college walls. When, as often happened, the weather became foul, this walking was crushed into the glass-house, a long corridor of glass-enclosed space which ran along the side of the main college buildings. Here boys were squashed into walking lines, which wheeled about at one end to begin the same walk all over again in monotonous repetition, with the steam of damp rising above their heads. Sometimes ranks were broken and groups tried to walk in the wrong direction, giving rise to fist fights and wrestling on the floor.

Hurling, that ancient, elegant game with hurley stick and leather ball, played between teams of fifteen aside, was at the centre of life in St Kieran's, a welcome relief from the monotony. You simply had to hurl or else sink into a corner, an object of derision. I felt a great sympathy for those boys who, for whatever reason, couldn't make it onto the hurling pitch. They were often sensitive and introspective, with an aversion to rough, physical play and they were mercilessly bullied by the others. In some respects I was one of them but I was also able to survive on the hurling pitch.

Each hurler had his own ash stick, which was measured by standing it at your side so that it came up to your hip bone. If it went higher or lower, it wasn't your size. Each hurley also sported its own distinctive markings. Maybe it was the way the hurley was strengthened with hoops of thin strips of tin, nailed to the wood of the butt of the hurley to make it stand up to the fierce clash of the ash on the field. When that tin stripping came loose in exchanges, as it inevitably did, it created another hazard for the players. Or, maybe, ownership of the hurley was indicated by how the handle was bound with black insulating tape to give it a better grip. Some boys gouged their initials into the side to ensure ownership. Whatever the markings, you had no difficulty in picking out your own hurley stick from the heap of sticks at the side of the field before training.

The hurling ball, or sliotar, is defined by its curious rim of raised leather on the surface. This makes it a deadly projectile as well as an effective item for handling and catching. Kilkenny players, particularly in defence, were, and still are today, known for their handling skills, catching the ball out of the sky in terrifying fashion with the clash of hurley sticks all around the frail, raised hand. There were also, always, those players who could direct the ball with malevolent accuracy towards different parts of an enemy's anatomy. We didn't wear helmets like present-day players, so part of the ritual of the game in school was the sporting of showy cuts, bruises and scars on the back of the head or hands the next day in the classroom.

The Kilkenny style, however, was never based upon brawn and muscle but upon the delicacy and speed of the players, who were characteristically light and small. Lifting the ball from the grass with the sharp edge of the butt of the stick, tossing it into the air and striking it cleanly without once touching the ball with the hand, a graceful movement of arms and hips – this was the central action. It was also an action that contrived to avoid the marker. There was something of a ghostly presence about all great Kilkenny forwards, like Jimmy Langton and Eddie Keher, now here, now there, gone, gliding past opponents and sending the ball neatly over the bar of the goalposts in the one smooth movement of play.

Across the county border in Tipperary you had a contrasting style, which produced some extraordinary battles between the two counties. Tipperary also had its stylish forwards, players of great physical grace, but the foundation of the typical Tipperary team was based upon rock-hard defence, tough backs who, in my day, proved particularly successful against the lighter Kilkenny forwards. Indeed, I was to experience this myself at college level. Was the term 'hair-oil hurlers' a Tipperary taunt, thrown at the stylish Kilkenny players, dancing at the edge of the action, looking great but getting nowhere in another Tipperary victory? Wherever it came from, the term summed up the stylishness of Kilkenny hurling.

Fennessy's Field behind the school, sharing a wall with the nearby Smithwick's brewery, was our testing ground and where the great St Kieran's teams of the 1940s and '50s were shaped and put together. It was also, of course, a nursery of the inter-county teams at the time. A great deal of tradition was passed on in the coaching. Our hurling trainer was a diminutive priest with a high quiff of greying hair falling to one side of his broad forehead. Father John Joe Reidy enjoyed another distinction before us boys: his brother Liam happened to play for the senior Kilkenny team. With a hurling stick in one hand and a lit cigarette in one corner of his mouth, Father Reidy ran up and down the sidelines yelling instructions at us on the field. He was an exacting trainer but clearly had a great love of the game and of his charges.

I remember his introduction of a hobbies club into the boarding school to help lift the tedium of those many wet days. He encouraged us to bring our stamp collections from home, thereby introducing something of the pleasure of home into the grim buildings of the school. He showed us how to build model aeroplanes, Spitfires and Messerschmidts, from balsa wood. We then flew them outdoors, propellers driven by tightly wound rubber bands, the best ones rising to heights and gliding back down again. Here was a priest who understood boys. Did he also choose the captain of the college Senior team?

In 1952 I was made captain of the St Kieran's Senior team. The All Ireland Colleges' Championship had been suspended in 1949 for reasons that have never been explained. But there was still the prized Leinster Championship and St Kieran's came to the championship in 1952 having won it on four previous, succeeding occasions. The school was now going for the five-in-a-row, so expectations were high, as was the degree of stress on the captain of the team. This was one of two times in my final years in the school when Father Reidy and his fellow priests gave me a position of responsibility. I think now that it might have been their way of boosting my self-esteem, which was never great in childhood.

On the hurling team I was positioned at right half-back and it was true I had some skills to qualify for the position. I could puck long high balls into the opponent's half. I was a sprinter and could reach the ball before many others. I could hook my marker's hurley stick from behind or charge it down from the front and block him from striking the ball. I could solo, at least for a short distance, with the ball balanced or bouncing on the butt of the hurley. I could even catch the incoming, dropping ball with my hand, although that was an activity I never enjoyed.

All this went for nought when St Kieran's met St Joseph's College, Roscrea, in the opening game of the competition. Kilkenny versus Tipperary all over again. For some reason, Roscrea, a Tipperary school, was then included in the Leinster and not the Munster championship. I was to make my first, close-up acquaintance with Tipperary hurling.

I found that the boy I was marking was the son of a friend of my father's and I think we spent a lot of the match in conversation. Serious mistake. Hurling, like every other game, is based upon a highly disciplined focus upon action. The mind of the player has to be rigorously controlled and, to a large degree, eliminated during the game. There is certainly no time for casual chat on the hurling field: anything that distracts from that focus is a weakness in the game. We were well beaten by Roscrea and that was the end of my hurling career. I may have played casual games of hurling with my brothers or my pals after this, but it was the last time I played a game in a competition.

Hurling has evolved from the relatively simple game that I remember in St Kieran's. For instance, there was much emphasis then on ground hurling, on quick, accurate hitting of the ball on the ground so that it might travel quickly from one end of the pitch to the other without once being lifted off the grass. You see very little of this anymore. Part of the evolution of the game has to do with the advance in fitness but it also has to do with tactics, which are well developed from those of Father Reidy.

I saw this development from high in the Hogan Stand at the 2008 All Ireland Final in Croke Park when Kilkenny gave the finest display of hurling that I have ever seen. Because of the elevation I could look down on the elaborate movements of the players, on and off the ball, that could be possible only with an advanced level of fitness training and coaching of high imagination. Was all this influenced by the patterns of soccer, particularly the decoy running off the ball?

The Kilkenny team on that day had, and still has, great individual players: Walsh, Delaney, Fitzpatrick, Shefflin, Brennan and a coach of genius in Brian Cody. But what was impressive was not individualism, although it was there in abundance, but the working of the team as a unit and at such a high level of efficiency. Watching the match, I remembered Father Reidy with affection. I cannot remember what he had to say to me after my disastrous captainship of his team but I doubt that it was hurtful. Whatever he said, he would have puffed away on the cigarette at the corner of his mouth the while, another sign of very different times and different ideas about taking care of the human body and getting it to perform to maximum effect.

In recent years I was invited back to St Kieran's to speak to the pupils at the annual prize-giving. There was little similarity to the school I had known in the past. It was an enjoyable experience, although I got a shock when I was reminded in public that I had captained the losing team in that match all those years before when St Kieran's had failed to make it five championships in a row. The ghost of Father Reidy, cigarette in the mouth, chuckled in the shadows.

Smoking in St Kieran's was prohibited for the rest of us but this only increased the desire to smoke. Complex systems of signalling and warning went on from group to group of the walkers around the college grounds. We used the schoolboy vernacular of nicknames and coded words as the stern prefect appeared in the distance, heading in our direction, dressed in his black coat, soutane and biretta. The biretta was a black, priestly hat, like a crown, with ridges and a tuft of black wool sticking out on top. Those caught smoking were told to turn up that evening at the dean's room for caning – 'six of the best' – on both palms. We used resin on our hurley sticks to protect them from breaking during games. We also used it on our hands to make the beatings slightly more bearable.

I turned back to St Kieran's in 2010 in the writing of my play *Christ Deliver Us!* for the Abbey Theatre. That play is loosely based upon Frank Wedekind's *Spring Awakening*, a play that has haunted me all my life, not only in its action but also through the story of the extraordinary presence of Wedekind himself as an actor-writer in the play's first production. *Spring Awakening* allowed me to write about St Kieran's, however obliquely. In 2010 much was made of the play's reflection of the ongoing debate on clerical scandals. I wasn't, however, trying to write about clerical sexual abuse.

One scene in that play came directly from my experience in a hall of St Kieran's. This is the scene where the boys are matched in pairs and given a lesson in how to waltz by the prefect-in-charge with the aid of a gramophone. It was the source of incredulous laughter in the Abbey Theatre. Of course it was ludicrous and I have no idea what was going through the mind of the cleric who thought it up. Certainly there would never be any question of inviting the girls from a local convent school to come along and take part in the dance lesson.

I never saw overt evidence of sexual abuse during my time in St Kieran's although the priests had favourites among the boys, called 'pets'. Caning on the hands was endemic, however. As the priests headed off to teach each morning, the bamboo cane was hanging from a button of the soutane or under the arm, a necessary item in the educational process, just as much as the books and papers that were used in the classroom. There was also a heavy strap of several layers of thick leather, which was a popular alternative punisher to the bamboo cane. Each priest and lay-teacher had a particular style of caning and some were fearsome; one individual, for instance, targeting the wrist, not the palm, with great accuracy.

What was the effect on these men of dishing out continuous beatings to young boys? There was no doubt that there were sadists among them. One priest would arrive in class on a Monday morning with a hearty greeting, 'What's the record now, lads?' The class would call out, 'Two hundred, Father,' this being the number of slaps delivered in the preceding week. 'We'll beat the record, lads, this week, so we will,' the priest announced and beat it he did on a regular basis so that the number of slaps that he delivered rose, week after week, like a feverish mathematics.

The truth is, of course, that the men were only repeating the physical abuse that they had suffered themselves as children and which was ingrained in Irish culture and a common feature of family life, as it was, indeed, in our own home. On the mantelpiece in our kitchen, when we were small, was a twig for punishment, more a threat than an actual weapon, it has to be said, but it was still used on small, bare legs from time to time.

This record-breaking priest was Father Jack Kennedy whose nickname was Syntax, as in Syntax Jack. His method of teaching Latin was based upon a personal invention of his, a survey of Latin syntax, which he dictated to the class. You had to write out this clear, simple structure of the language in a special copy-book that could not be used for any other purpose. On the cover you wrote *Syntax* in bold lettering and you never forgot the contents. This was how I learned grammar. This was how I learned how a sentence is assembled and the purposes of its various clauses. It seemed a natural passage from the lines and columns of syntax in Father Jack's notebook to the writing of English. We were often hungry in St Kieran's but, unknown to ourselves, we were being fed on other food.

This was Ireland in the immediate post-war years when money and food were severely limited. We trooped in a line into the large refectory of St Kieran's at mealtimes, one section full of ecclesiastical students in black soutanes and white Roman collars, the rest full of lay boys, all at long tables. A prefect sat at the top of each of the boys' tables. Strict silence was imposed during eating and, to ensure this, a senior priest walked up and down between the rows reading his breviary but with one eye on the proceedings. At a lectern in the middle of the refectory a chosen ecclesiastic read monotonously from some book or other of a deadly, spiritual nature, lives of the saints and the like.

I remember little of the food except that it was mostly disgusting. There was one concoction of eggs watered down so that it would feed a hungry horde. Bread was often stale or mouldy, and word was that the college and the Kilkenny lunatic asylum shared a contract with a local baker for leftovers. One rice dessert was known among the boys as frogspawn, while the watery egg dish was called a variety of lavatorial names.

There was at least one protest. On that occasion, for some reason, there was no prefect at one of the tables. Instead, a tough senior schoolboy presided at the top. When the plates were filled with whatever stuff was on offer, this boy took his full plate and dumped it back into the serving bowl. Everyone at the table followed suit and soon there was a high pile of dirty plates sticking out of the bowl with food streaming all over the table. The priest on duty was in a rage. He dragged the big youngster, who was almost as big as himself, to the centre of the refectory and screamed abuse at him. Mention was made of the starving black babies of Africa. The boy was made to stand. The red-faced priest rushed out and returned quickly with a cane and proceeded to give double punishment to the boy, six strokes on each hand, instead of the usual three. For a moment afterwards it looked as if the boy was about to strike the priest but that didn't happen.

Because of the pressure to find enough food, the college actively encouraged the boys' parents to send in supplementary food from home. Each boy had to have a tuck box, a wooden box with the name of the owner painted across it and with its own padlock. These boxes were piled high outside the refectory in a corridor that stank constantly of decaying food. The area, dark and foul-smelling, was known, appropriately enough for a classics-based school, as Hades.

So each week a battered brown suitcase arrived for my brothers and myself at the college gate from Tom Nolan's Callan bus. We picked it up, excitedly, at the front gates. In it was the clean laundry for the week, washed by our mother, with a pound of creamery butter from the Callan Co-op and a variety of food, mostly my mother's baking, including her delicious currant buns. The feeding of the boys around the tuck boxes was savage, unsupervised, a place of gorging, which, it seemed, the priests and prefects had surrendered to the hungry boys.

I have often wondered about that surrender of control around the tuck boxes. Was it some kind of guilt on the part of the school authorities, unable to feed their charges properly? No priest or prefect ever came near, as far as I remember, while the boys tore open packages of ham and hard-boiled eggs, home-made cakes and bags of apples or plums, and walked the food refuse into the ground under their feet. For a while the richness of the Kilkenny countryside came into our walled school and the homesickness became unbearable. But it is the image of animal feeding that remains with me now.

Whatever about its deficiencies and discomforts, St Kieran's, like the other Catholic boarding schools around the country, was educating one of the first generations of rural Irish boys to receive a secondary education. It was remarkable, if schematic, in content and revolutionary in its effects. It had two distinguishing features. One was five years of Greek and Latin. The other was that you could take several subjects through the Irish language and thus have your mark raised by twenty per cent. This meant that you could end up with a 120 per cent result in Greek or Latin. This actually happened more than once in St Kieran's.

I was in the place for six years, not the usual five. To go to university I had to win one of the few competitive County Council Scholarships offered in the Leaving Certificate examination at the end of five years. I failed to do so at the first attempt but managed it the second time around. In this way I read not only the *Philoctetes* of Sophocles but the first and *Second Philippics* of Demosthenes as well. Slaving through the texts, line by line, I had little sense of the vision of these works. Yet, still, something of the clear, humanist values of a classical education came through, particularly in episodes outside the curriculum itself. This was when the boys exploited the weaknesses of the priests and lay teachers, distracting them from the regulation texts.

Father Tommy Brennan (whose nickname was Tommy the Rule) could be sidetracked easily from the examination texts with a few well-chosen, innocently faced questions about Greek culture. 'Will you tell us about Greek theatre, Father?' 'Ah, now, lads, we should be doing the translation, so we should!' But Tommy the Rule wandered off talking about Greek civilization with such passion that I immediately saw the white sunlit temples, the olive groves, the walking figures disputing on the marble floors, the sailing ships setting out on those fabulous journeys into the sunshine of the Aegean Sea. The struggle between Athenian and Spartan was a mythical one of opposing human values, spiritual versus physical, the humane civilization of Athens, the martial, physical culture of Sparta. The battles to keep out the Persians by the Greeks at Thermopylae and Marathon were turning points in the struggle to prevent the alien forces of the Orient from invading Europe.

Poor Father Brennan knew about this cultural history, although its issues never appeared on examination papers. He couldn't resist talking about this classical heritage despite his immense worry about wasting time. 'Ah, lads,' he would cry, his broad face creased with anxiety, 'will ya look at the time, with the day wasted and the Leaving just round the corner!' But he must also have had a sense of the valuable education he was imparting to us on the side. Of course he was always careful to remark that whatever the value of this classical humanism, these people were still 'pagans'. Somewhere, in this extracurricular lesson of Father Brennan, was the one that Christianity took what was best from the Greeks and Romans, transmitting classical civilization to Europe and leaving the paganism behind.

I promised myself in the classroom of St Kieran's that I would go and see these places of beauty for myself one day – Delphi, Marathon and the Parthenon – with those incredible stories attached to them. I made the journey while still a student in Dublin, in 1956. I went via Tito's Yugoslavia, on a dark train journey, eventually crossing Macedonia and arriving in Athens. I returned, never the same again, crossing the Mediterranean from Piraeus in Greece to Brindisi in southern Italy, then hitch-hiking home through Italy and France and across Britain to the boat train for Ireland at Holyhead.

Another more enlightened priest, Father Peter Birch, who taught us English, did something similarly remarkable and off the curriculum. As part of his teaching of Shakespearean tragedy he brought in a translation of the first *stasimon* or choral ode of the *Antigone* of Sophocles. He showed us how that great hymn to the wonders of humankind anticipated a similar celebration of humanity in *Hamlet* and with much the same mixture of humanist celebration and a tragic recognition of evil.

Father Birch drew our attention to the Greek word *deina* and its complexity of meanings. Yes, it meant wonders, as in the *deina* of human capabilities, but it also meant horrors. There was no English word to convey this clash of meanings and therefore no single word in English, as there is in Greek, to transmit the dual impact of tragedy, the wonderful and the monstrous, in human character. Father Birch talked about tragedy combining the human capacity to rise to great heights and the weakness to fall into the pit. The play *Antigone* may contain one of the great celebrations of human perfection in literature but it is also a play containing human savagery, incest, fratricide, a putrefying corpse, live immurement in a cave and a triple suicide. Like all great lessons in literature, this one of Birch's was also a lesson about life.

An elegant, stylish priest, Father Birch went on to become that rare phenomenon in Irish life, a radical bishop with a passionate interest in the fate of the dispossessed and the mentally ill. As I watched his work over the years, an enlightened figure in a seemingly unreformable and secretly corrupt institution, I remembered his loneliness and isolation all those years before in St Kieran's. Each weekend he would get into his car and escape to Dublin. There he had friends like the convivial Benedict Kiely, whose novels, at the time, were banned in Ireland for 'indecency'. Birch gave me Kiely's book *Modern Irish Fiction* to read and I suddenly discovered that literature didn't end in the nineteenth century, as it did in the school syllabus. In particular, I discovered Joyce, at one remove it is true, and began at once to try and get my hands on the Joyce books themselves. Ben Kiely was to become a friend of mine when I reached Dublin and we often talked about Birch.

A lay teacher, John Wilson, taught me how to structure and develop an essay and how to employ definition in an opening paragraph. He didn't spend a long time in St Kieran's and eventually went on to become a prominent politician and deputy prime minister of his country, renowned for his florid oratorical style and classical quotations in the Dáil.

At St Kieran's John Wilson was celebrated as an inter-county footballer, playing for his native Cavan in the 1947 All Ireland Final against Kerry. The match was famous in that it was played at the old Polo Grounds in New York, partly to mark the centenary of the Irish Famine. As excited schoolboys, we were only conscious of the exotic fact that one of our teachers was engaged in a football match in America. The truth was that Wilson had a torrid time on the pitch trying to cope with the Kerry star Batt Garvey. It was only when Cavan mentors made a switch, replacing Wilson, that they won the match. Back in Kilkenny, however, Wilson was still our hero.

Transformative education seemed to creep in like this through cracks in the institution, almost accidental exposure to the world beyond the walls of the college. Sometimes this was contact, however awkwardly, with great art. Each year the ecclesiastic students performed a Shakespearean play. Some effort was made in production values and costumes were hired from Dublin and London. We lay boys were part of the audience. I had seen Shakespearean productions by travelling fit-up companies back home in the Callan parochial hall. The ecclesiastical productions of Shakespeare were more a demonstration of the hazards of amateur acting and the spectacle of priestly students in drag. We took a particular, revengeful delight in seeing our prefects on stage making fools of themselves, as we thought.

On one occasion the world of fit-up theatre actually entered our classroom. Some other imaginative priest arranged to have the great actor-manager Anew McMaster address our Leaving

Certificate English class. Perhaps it was the same Father Birch? I don't think so but I have a sense that it was the priest who produced the ecclesiastic Shakespearean production. McMaster must have been performing with his troupe in Kilkenny. I didn't know it, of course, but Harold Pinter was touring Ireland with the McMaster company at around this time, playing Horatio, Macduff, Iago, Sir Robert Chiltern and John Worthing as he describes in his charming memoir *Mac*.

We were studying *Hamlet* with Birch. McMaster sat on a chair before the class of eighteen-year-old boys, one hand floating in an airy gesture. We had never seen anything like him in all our short lives: dyed, tossed blond hair, the daytime make-up clearly visible around the glaring blue eyes, the elegant tweed suit, the contrasting flowery waistcoat and that voice, oh, that voice! The only way I can describe his 'performance' is that he 'took' us through *Hamlet*. Not the whole play, although much of what he offered was a cliff-hanging narrative of the plot, an aspect of the play that has stayed with me ever since. But he did act out several parts as well, from a simpering Ophelia to a grumpy Polonius and, everywhere possible, a youthful, charismatic Prince. The years fell away from the actor in the chair in front of our eyes. It was my first experience up close of great acting and a demonstration that such talent could theatricalize any space, that theatre, given the talent, can happen anywhere, even in a broom closet. Or a school classroom.

It was also my first encounter with the element of the monstrous in great acting, although I couldn't articulate this at the time. Nevertheless, I was conscious of my fear in the presence of McMaster, a fear that was thrilling in its intensity. While the performance was unmistakably human, it had also passed beyond the usual human restraints of decorum and control, creating a figure of outlandish proportions. Most theatrical performances slip out of the mind along with the other debris of daily life but this kind of performance is indelible. You will never forget it because of this element of the monstrous in its make-up.

The actor and the priest both need a stage, a text, a costuming, a performance and an audience. The most incisive account of this kinship is to be found in a brilliant essay, 'The Priest and the Jester' by the Polish philosopher Leszek Kolakowski. 'The priest is the guardian of the absolute,' as Kolakowski puts it; 'the jester is the impertinent upstart who questions everything.' Kolakowski's essay is not limited to religion and dissent from belief, although he has many interesting things to say about the power and energy of religion and its contribution to European culture, the way theology continues to haunt Western philosophy, even in a secular age.

In the end, his essay is about a constant, a universal opposition in human nature, of two opposing world views ingrained in human thought, one championing orthodoxy, which might be religious or Marxist or that of any other ideology, the other reducing everything to a comic, common denominator. In effecting this dialectic, Kolakowski brings the priest and the actor into close intimacy, but an intimacy that forbids a coming together, disallowing a resolution because they represent the essential, divided, tragic nature of the way of the world: 'Both the priest and the jester violate the mind: the former by strangling it with catechism, the latter by harassing it with mockery. At a royal palace there are more priests than jesters – just as in a king's realm there are more policemen than artists. It does not seem possible to change this.'

What is interesting to me here, looking back on my childhood, is the implication throughout Kolakowski's essay that both priest and jester are performers on a chosen stage with the public as audience, the prize being authority through control and persuasion. Not only do the priest and jester each require a performance space and routine, each requires costuming, a motley, to distinguish himself from the public. Without that public, each of them would remain inarticulate.

As altar boys, we were privy to the priestly role on the altar. It was so striking a role to me as a child that it became part of my childhood play. On the narrow staircase of our house on Green

View Terrace I played at being a priest with the first few steps of the stairs as my altar.

What is surprising is that far from being shocked at such impiety, my mother collaborated in it and got my sisters to help. Old bibs and scarves were found, which could be used as vestments, an old tin cup became the ciborium. The younger brothers were dragooned into playing altar boys and the sisters were told to Hush! as the bell rang out and I turned and raised a piece of white paper as host to my congregation in the kitchen. It was long before I had that aspiration to become a Franciscan friar. Could my mother have had the hope that this activity might be an indication of an incipient vocation to the priesthood, the hope of all Irish mothers to have 'a priest in the family'? In truth it was my first, very early, performance upon a stage. Maybe she found it comic? Like many people given to depression, she considered much of life hilarious.

I have one other memory of that stairs, which may be my earliest memory. I was very, very small and the memory comes from the shock of medication. I am in my mother's arms, a bundle of feverish heat and irritation, bawling loudly. She was carrying me downstairs so that our neighbour, Mrs Barry, who knew about such things, could make an inspection of me at the bottom of the stairs. I had been inoculated on my right arm against one or other of the flaming fevers that raged through my childhood and the inoculation hadn't taken well. I was scratching the scab and my hand flew out and scratched my mother's face. What was my problem had now become much more serious and Mrs Barry was trying to attend to the ugly, toxic scratch on my mother's cheek. Years later she would still show me, with a laugh, the scar from it.

As a schoolboy in St Kieran's College I came very close to the theatricality of religion. I remained a pious believer, so that my latent disbelief never surfaced, but I remember the religious experience now as an act of theatre, a performance for effect. The fact that this is the way I now see it in memory must mean that I was already a doubter below the surface back in St Kieran's.

This intimacy with religion was further intensified in my case because the priests singled me out as a figure who represented their authority among the boys. Each year two boys were chosen from the Final Leaving Certificate Honours class as head boys of the school. They were called First Senior and Second Senior. The idea was that they would represent school authority to the boys, report problems and complaints to the priests and in general act as links in the chain of power, which kept the place under strict control. I was the First Senior in my final year. It was a lesson in the nature of power over others. After communal events, the daily mass in chapel, after each meal in the refectory, my colleague and I led the line of hundreds of boys, two by two, towards the exit. I must have been insufferable.

One other duty of the First and Second Seniors was to go to the College President in the company of two senior ecclesiastical students to ask for a 'free' day. The occasion might be after a particular win in a hurling match or to honour boys who had performed well in the state examinations or to celebrate the visit of an archbishop or a cardinal to the ecclesiastical side of the college.

The whole place lay hushed in silence with great excitement, the boys sitting in their classrooms whispering, the priests and lay teachers awaiting the outcome in the teachers' room. My fellow senior and myself stood at the archway where we were joined by the two ecclesiastics.

We four then climbed the polished staircases to the top of the front of college and the rooms of Canon Dunphy, the President, whose nickname was The Bear. He was a tall, gaunt, bald man with black bushy eyebrows and a forbidding exterior, which actually concealed a gentle, compassionate creature. He addressed everyone in a harsh Mooncoin accent as 'me man'. 'What is it now, me man?' he demanded grimly of the ecclesiastic who led us to the door, although he must have known very well why we were there. Sometimes we were sent packing with a roar from The Bear. But usually we raced down the stairs shouting 'Free Day!

Free Day!' At the archway once more we rang the school bell in triumph and I can still hear the huge roar of repressed energy that followed and the rush of boys out into the open air.

There are two other memories of my function as First Senior, which involved an intimacy with priests that gave me an insight into the all-too-human figure behind the priestly role. One memory had to do with bullying. One form of bullying in St Kieran's was called 'stretching' and it must have been a dangerous activity for the victim. He was thrown to the ground on his back and four boys took hold of his legs and outstretched hands. The four boys pulled and the victim was 'stretched', not once but several times. The bullying ended with the victim being bounced against the ground, up and down, up and down. I have no idea where this 'stretching' came from but it did have some resemblance to the rack of the Inquisition. Nor have I any memory of dislocated shoulders, but I do remember the screams. Sometimes 'stretching' was meted out to 'pets' of the priests.

One night, after lights out, in my final year, I was visited in our dormitory by one of the younger priests, a nervous, thin individual who stood at the end of my bed beside the window. In the senior dormitory we each had timber cubicles giving us a degree of privacy. The priest whispered and played with the cord of the roller blind on the window behind him, toying with the cord as he pitched his strange request to me.

I was to remember this scene some years later when I first read *A Portrait of the Artist as a Young Man.* I was reminded of it when I read of the director of the college in the shadows by the window, running the cord of the blind through his fingers as he tempted Stephen with the allure of the power of the priesthood. Back in St Kieran's my priest had a more practical purpose. He spoke with a grieving face of the 'stretching' of his 'pet', although he didn't use that word. He said he knew I could influence the perpetrators. Could I do something to stop it? I can't remember how things turned out but I have a feeling that I rescued the unfortunate victim. I do remember, though, how I reacted to the priest. I positively glowed with self-importance in the bed. I never thought of the strangeness of the event. All that mattered was that the priest had elevated me in importance by taking me into his confidence in this way.

The second such close encounter with the priesthood had to do with the celebration of a Solemn High Mass in the college chapel where I played the role of master of ceremony. A Solemn High Mass in St Kieran's was a big deal, reserved for very special occasions, a particular saint's feast day, for example. The celebrating priest and his attendant deacon and sub-deacon were dressed up in gilt vestments. A full choir of attendant priests contributed to the responses in Gregorian chant. It was immensely impressive. In the body of the church the full complement of ecclesiastical and lay students turned out for the event and there was always a special breakfast served afterwards.

How on earth was I chosen as master of ceremony? Perhaps the First Senior of the day was always given the job? Maybe a boy was chosen as a potential candidate for the priesthood? Whatever the reason, there I was in full soutane and elaborate white surplice together with the roman collar. It was as near as you could get to the role of priesthood itself without being ordained. Indeed most masters of ceremony at a High Mass were priests or students close to ordination.

I must have been schooled well in advance because the master of ceremony is required to have a thorough knowledge of the liturgy of the service. In effect, he directs the different moves of the ritual upon the altar. Clapping is used to draw attention to a new move within the sanctuary. I remember being dazed throughout by the sheer display of it all and the overwhelming smell of incense, burning candlewax and wine, which contributed to the honeyed intimacy of the figures on the altar.

There was another potent smell, one of washed and soaped males in close proximity to one another, a slight whiff of perspiration as everyone was under stress to perform without mishap, up and down the altar steps, back and forth before the tabernacle in that astonishing action at the heart of the ritual, the claimed transformation of bread and wine into the body and blood of Christ. I remember the difficulty in performing my actions, the closeness of the space, the intimacy of the bodies on the altar, the smell of laundered vestments.

What I most remember of all on that altar, however, were the moments of exclusion. I was there but I wasn't there. As a lay master of ceremony I was, in those days, forbidden to handle the sacred vessels – the paten, the chalice, the ciborium – although they glittered in gold and silver right in front of me. Whenever the point was reached to move the vessels, the blessed hands of the priest and deacon intervened and firmly moved the objects out of my reach.

At those moments I must have sensed the essential absurdity at the heart of priesthood. I knew these men as ordinary, fallible, in some cases very weak, mortals. It must have struck me with force that an elaborate piece of theatricality was claiming for them a direct access to a divinity, above and beyond the reach of ordinary people. Being this close to the action broke the mystery, although it was to be some time before I was able to throw off the shackles completely. The irony is that this freedom from religion, when it did come, would reach me through theatre.

It was in St Kieran's, too, that I first learned details of the late war. One history teacher devoted a whole class to tracing the movements of the combatants across the maps. This was an unusual step, since it was a distraction from the examination syllabus and would be looked upon by the school authorities as a waste of time. When someone asked the history teacher about the Jews, however, he became evasive. He seemed far more interested in warning us about the Red Peril of the Soviets and their takeover of parts of Europe. It was as if the only meaning to be drawn from the war was the opportunity it had given to the dreaded communists to take control of Eastern Europe.

It was about this time, too, that I became aware of the number of Germans who had moved to Ireland immediately after the war. Very few of them stayed for long but they brought with them a sense of the great dramatic happenings across the seas. My childhood was in a small-town, provincial setting, in many ways cut off from a wider, European experience, but this was one of the ways in which this larger experience poured into my consciousness as a child. This was how, too, I became aware of the ambivalent attitudes of Irish people towards the war and towards Germans. Some of this was fuelled by anti-English sentiment; some of it came out of traditional service in the British army. I had no doubt about such matters. Germany had released profound evil in Europe during the war and that was that. I had great trouble meeting these German visitors.

Cromwell had entered my imagination through the games we had played in the fair green behind our house. Hitler also entered my consciousness but through my observation of the German settlers. I remember the distaste with which I looked upon these people. Some of them must have been innocent of wrongdoing, although I was bothered by the fact that they were well off, at least compared to ourselves and our neighbours. They were certainly far removed from the haggard refugees we had watched in the newsreels of the local cinema.

When I turn now to this second piece of fiction, I am using it to imagine the way in which another great external, historical event touched upon the town. It is like my story of the two boys and the Cromwellian siege but it is also different. This is a fiction set during my own lifetime. It is the story of a local girl and boy and their encounters with a German couple. There is little that is personal in it and there is no resemblance between the German couple and any couple I have ever met. It may rely upon the confusion about sexuality that I felt as youngster. I have also drawn from the personal in one, other detail. I have imagined an elderly man looking back upon his childhood from a great distance. There is memory here, then, but memory refracted through the imagination.

7

THE ARRIVAL OF HITLER

A Fictional Interlude

People seeing me today in my late seventies on my sedate, daily walk would hardly think of me as someone who is carrying a secret story of passion along with my walking stick. They would hardly associate me with heartbreak. Cautious behaviour in all things, financial as well as emotional, yes, but not crushing grief at the loss of love, no, nothing like that. That would not fit with my prim, spotless exterior, coat and hat, dressed to deter the elements. Yet there has hardly been a week in the past sixty-six years of my life in which I haven't thought of Livie.

Features of my present life, which may connect the 'me' that I am now to the 'me' that I was back then, all those years ago: I still dislike (I almost said heartily) the Germans, I am still squeamish at the sight of blood, I still wear glasses but now they are so heavy they have grooved my nose, I still read dictionaries for pleasure. And I am alone.

I also have affection for the child I was then, that fat little boy with his endless questions, but I cannot understand how he relates to the adult I have become. He belongs to a different place.

He even speaks a different language. He is like a distant, minia-ture relative, instead of my own, walking DNA.

I have also moved so far away from the town that I grew up in that it requires a big effort of invention to go back there anymore. It was what used to be called 'a garrison town', that is, one that housed a military barracks when the British occupied the country before independence. Maybe that explained the ambiguous attitude locally to the Germans. For a place that turned quickly against any outsiders, the odd, stray foreigner and the like, the locals had an ambivalent attitude to the German cause during the war. There was a great deal of sympathy for the Nazis. This may account for the welcome that the German couple got when they arrived in the place and caused such commotion in Livie's heart. In our house, though, things were different. My father told us that the Germans were the baddies.

I tell myself now that what I lost in Livie would have been lost anyway in my becoming what I have become, the successful clerk, the guardian of other people's money. Can't turn back the clock and all the rest of that clichéd rubbish. Livie could never have had a place in the life that I have lived since then, certainly not.

None of this, though, is of the slightest help to me in trying to cope with the pain. If anything, it makes things worse. On my own, I continue to shake and shudder at the memory of what happened all those years ago. There is the conviction as well that, for a brief few months, I was given sight of something precious, something with incredible promise before it was snatched away from me.

It was just a few years after the end of World War II. The town had not really been touched by it, despite the way some people cheered the defeats of Britain. The war was out there and far away, in places with strange names.

When I think now of my childhood, I think of the town as like the castle in the fairy tale, covered in undergrowth, with its inhabitants awaiting the kiss of the prince and princess so that they might wake up again.

Livie told me stories of the war years, even though she must have been too young herself to experience very much of them. She told me about the lone fighter aircraft that came over the town one evening, swooping and looping over the rooftops as if the pilot were trying to find out where he was. Everyone came out onto the street, she said, to watch the great, grey, mechanical bird.

I watched her excitement as she said all this to me, the quiver of her lips, the gasp of her breath. I could watch that long white face, those large blue eyes for ever and ever. The Cross was packed with people, she said, that evening. I wanted to touch her face then, I wanted to touch her excitement with my fingertips, but I hadn't the nerve. No one could be certain, she said, whether it was a Tommy or a Jerry plane, or even a Yank gone astray from up in the northern Six Counties.

Livie had gone out of my life by the time the German couple were to leave the place again, selling up and sneaking away to some other hideaway or maybe back to where they came from in the first place. Who knows? So I couldn't talk to her about what had happened. I never got the chance to ask her what they did to her that night when the German men took her into the Butler House.

All I was left with was the memory of her up in the tree. A lanky, pale fifteen-year-old in a dirty yellow dress with a tear at one hem. Her long arms and long legs were all over the place and didn't seem to be connected, as if there were several different girls up there in the branches and the leaves and not just one Livie, my Livie. I was eleven years old. I already knew too much about the carry-on of grown-ups. I also didn't know enough to calm my terrors, which were ferocious.

Livie loved the pictures. Her favourite was the comedian Joe E. Brown with the big mouth of teeth, although she was partial, too, to cowboys. She'd go two or three times a week to the Gaiety Cinema on Line Street, if she was let and cash permitting. On her own, in one of the back rows, she informed me. Sometimes, she said, a fella might invite himself to join her there.

'What for?'

'God Almighty, Andrew, you're the limit, so y'are!'

'Why so?'

'Ask me no questions,' she chanted as if about to break into song, ''n I'll tell ya no lies. 'Sides, there's a snot comin' down outta yer nose.'

'Is not!' I countered, hurt, but I wiped my nose on the sleeve of my jersey just to be on the safe side.

I was allowed to go to the pictures only on the odd matinee and to dumb stuff by the likes of Walt Disney, so the rituals of cinema-going were still a mystery to me. Whenever Livie was mad with me, she called me Andrew instead of the usual Andy. I felt a terrible shame at not being able to go to the pictures whenever I wanted.

'They won't let me go to the pictures at home. They say they're not good for me.'

'Why don't ya steal the feckin' money outta yer mother's purse when she's not lookin'? I would.'

'That'd be stealin', so 'twould.'

'I know that, ya eejit, isn't that what I've been sayin'? Stealin'. God give me patience with ya!'

She loved using grown-up phrases like this. I knew that sometimes she was trying to imitate the way the nuns talked in the convent school.

Usually our talks about the pictures ended with her suggesting a game of make-believe, based upon something she had seen on the screen. I loved those games with her. They were like being transported inside the covers of a comic book, *The Beano* or *The Hotspur*. Livie's inventiveness knew no bounds.

'Let's pretend we're beyond in the desert! You could be the Arab with the camel standin' to wan side, like. I could be the maiden with the scarf down over me face, the wan that the sheikh was after all the time.'

'How could we do that?'

'Excuse me, Mister Useless! I forget ya weren't at the pictures the other night. I should be talkin' to somewan else, somewan grown up and not some snotty young lad.'

'Am not a snotty young lad, so I'm not.'

'Well, then! Act like yer not. I think I'll go to America like the Barry twins. Here! Let me straighten yer glasses for ya. Lookit the way they're fallin' down yer nose.'

She was always grabbing something of mine, my shirt or my glasses or whatever, to straighten me out, as she put it. Usually this annoyed the hell out of me as it made me feel small. But, sometimes, to my shock, I felt a shudder of what appeared to be delight running right through my system when she manhandled me in this fashion. At times like these, I thought there was no one in the wide world like Livie.

Right now, without another word, she whipped off my glasses and started to twist and turn them with her fingers in an alarming fashion. Her tongue stuck out as it usually did whenever she was concentrating upon a job in hand. Usually when people stuck out their tongues, it was a sign of rudeness. Or it made them ugly. Not Livie. I could watch her intent, small red tongue for ever, moving like a creature on its own inside her. I was fearful, though, for the glasses.

'Don't break them! I'm blind as a bat without them.'

'You see more than is good for ya already, young fella.'

Watching my chance, I grabbed the glasses from her before she could do further damage. But she was already distracted. That was another thing about Livie: she never stayed with any one thing for very long but moved onto something else like a white bird landing. I shoved the glasses back over my eyes but, as usual, they started sliding down my nose again. Pushing them back up again, sliding down again, pushing them back up again. I hated those bloody glasses with a vengeance.

My mother and the two sisters had a dim view of Livie. Fortunately they had no notion of how often I was meeting up with her, out on the fair green or down the river. They said Livie was 'common'. I asked them what did they mean by that, knowing full well that the two sisters were only repeating the word after my mother and probably didn't know what they were talking about. My mother said I'd know more when I'd grow up. One of the sisters said Livie's father was beyond in a factory in England, as if that explained everything.

There was a small dictionary in the house that my father used when he did the crossword in the paper. My father was a clerk in O'Brien's the solicitors and never said much. My mother thought it was the most important job in the town. I thought otherwise.

I spent a lot of time with my head in that dictionary, mostly tracking down words that I had heard from the adults. Sometimes in the search I got distracted and spun off into other words on the page that were mysterious and magical.

I found the word 'common'. 'Ordinary' or 'usual', it said, which didn't take me far. But, then, down below in the second or third meanings, which I always loved to rummage in because of their surprises, I found the word 'vulgar'. I was shocked. Livie wasn't vulgar. She might use the word feck now and again but she was really special. She had a small cluster of freckles on either side of her nose but, otherwise, in my book, she was near perfect.

I told my mother and sisters that I was going to marry Livie. 'If I can catch up with her,' I said, meaning the age difference between us. They just hooted with laughter. I didn't care. I had given myself, heart and soul, to Livie and that was that. Even though I was only eleven, I felt protective of her, which was one of the reasons I was so shattered by how things turned out. I was made to feel that I had failed her on that awful night, running off the way I did.

'Ya can't go to America without an X-ray,' I told her on the subject of her plans to emigrate like the Barrys.

'A wha'?'

'X-ray. Ya know? Picturing yer insides. For to make sure ya don't have the TB.'

We had a cousin who went to Boston to be a maid in a house. I was very impressed by the hullabaloo of her departure with the big brown envelope under her oxter. 'Don't bend it now!' every one called out to her as she got on the bus to go to the Kilkenny railway station. 'Keep it flat at all costs 'til ya get past the entrance to America.'

'My dear child,' said Livie, 'ya don't know what yer talkin' about.' (See what I mean about that nun talk?) 'Maybe I'll go to Australia instead.' She always had an answer to everything, Livie.

'Get yer togs, Andy!' When Livie gave this order I knew we were going swimming down the river.

It was one of the days my mother took in washing to make a little extra money. Steam rose about herself and the two sisters in the back kitchen, so they paid no attention to me when I said I was going out to play. My mother had a cloth tied around her head so that the bones on her face stood out more than usual. She just looked at me vacantly. I didn't like seeing her tired like that even at the start of the day. I snuck out the front door, my togs rolled up in an old towel and stuck up under my jersey, not to give the game away.

It was early on a Saturday morning, so we had the river to ourselves with an odd bullock in the fields. Sometimes Livie wore her togs under her dress. Sometimes she went off into the next meadow to change while I struggled with the old towel around my waist, trying to get my trousers off and the togs on without losing my decency. I was starting to get fatter along with all my other worries into the bargain.

After the swim, we lay down on the bank and dried ourselves in the pale sun. I wasn't paying her much attention. I was still worried about my mother and the washing. It didn't seem right, somehow, enjoying myself like this while she slaved at home in the sweltering back kitchen. Suddenly Livie jumped up and started to walk away without a word.

'Where ya goin', miss?'

'Miss! Who're ya callin' miss, young fella. Mind yer manners, you!' Then she was gone.

'Livie?'

'Andy!' she called, but from a distance.

'Wha'?'

'Come here!'

'What for?'

'Never mind. Come here, will ya! This instant, now!'

I put on my glasses and set off. She must be in the meadow with the high grass.

'Where are ya?'

'Over here!'

I waded through the high grass, walking slowly in her direction. There she was, without a stitch on her, no togs or nothing. I stopped in my tracks.

'Come here, will ya and stop gawpin'.'

The biggest shock was how small and thin she was. Even in her togs I always thought of Livie as big – much bigger than me. Here she was now with this straight, thin white body, the thin arms and thin legs. It was only after minutes that I took in the rest, the small patch of hair at the top of her legs, the nipples and the faint outline of breasts. I had seen all this before in pictures in books but it was all different on Livie.

She shook her head vigorously. She had a habit of doing this when about to launch herself in some devilment, like climbing over a wall to steal apples in Lyons's orchard, shaking her brown curls loose so that they came down over her forehead, nearly covering her eyes. She did this now but, instead of making her look bold, it only made her seem helpless. I wanted to say something nice to her but I couldn't think of anything. Besides, I was in a state of shock.

'Take down yer togs,' she ordered in a husky kind of voice.

'I dunno,' I said.

'Go on! Before someone comes! Do what yer told, young lad!'

I looked around me. No one in sight, not even the cattle. I looked down at my old, worn black togs. I put my thumbs under the elastic and rolled them down. When I came to the knees, I wobbled. Then I stepped out of them and rolled the togs fiercely into a ball with one fist. I couldn't look at her. I hoped I didn't look too fat.

'I'm going to turn me back now,' she said and she did. She looked even thinner from behind. Her bottom was small, no bigger than two large apples. I had seen bottoms before, once in a book, but none as small as Livie's. She turned back again, again with a slight toss of her curls.

'You turn round now,' she ordered. 'Go on! Turn round.'

I turned slowly. I knew I was blushing and when I looked down at my belly I was shocked to see that it was coloured too. Maybe I was blushing all over? I turned back again quickly.

'Your thing will get bigger,' she said as if to cheer me up. I knew what she was talking about. I looked down at myself. I never called it 'my thing'. I called it 'my wee-wee' because that was what my mother called it. 'Now, Andy, we have to wash your wee-wee,' she'd say at bathtime. If anything, it now seemed to be getting smaller and smaller by the minute.

'Why?' I asked, choking on the word. At first I didn't know what question I was asking. I gulped again. 'Why will it get bigger?' I said then after a few seconds just to fill up the silence.

'For to fit in here,' she answered and she put a hand on the hair between her legs, watching me carefully all the while. She left her hand on the hair for a moment or two and then parted her fingers. I saw the flash of pink flesh between her fingers and I thought my knees were finished.

'That's enough now.' Something of her old bossy voice had come back to her again. 'Put yer togs back on, Andy. Go on now,' she said, 'back to the riverbank, with ya. Go on now. I'll be there in a while.'

I did as I was told with shaky fingers and feet. I couldn't look in her direction again. I wished there was someone I could tell what had happened to me. But I knew I couldn't tell anyone and certainly not my mother. She'd have conniptions.

Then suddenly I remembered confession. I was terrified once again because I was going to have to confess all this next time to the priest in the confession box. Back on the riverbank I practised confession a few times in my head. I often rehearse things like this, especially when I land in trouble and have to talk my way out of it.

'Bless me, Father, for I have sinned. I seen a naked girl.'

'Did you have any part in any of this carry-on?'

'No, Father. She took her clothes off be herself.'

'And what happened?'

'Nothing, Father. What I mean is she tauld me to take me togs off as well, an' I did.'

'To take off your what?'

'Me swimming togs, Father.'

'And what is this girl's name? Answer me!'

I'd try to get Father Casey the curate in the confession box because he was a cinch at it. He only ever wanted a rough idea of what happened and never asked for specifics. But if I was forced to go into the confession box of Canon Dooley, the parish priest, I was a goner. He'd have to hear everything. He'd certainly ask her name, but how could I betray Livie? I stayed away from confession for several weeks and finally found a visiting friar in the friary who had no interest in my adventure down the river.

When did Livie get to know the German couple the way she did? How did she worm her way into being best pals with Mrs Gerber? She was certainly there with the rest of us at the side gate of Butler House when we watched the three big lorries unloading all the German stuff on the driveway by the front door. Furniture, big pictures with huge frames and boxes of all kinds, trunks, tea chests and smaller cardboard boxes. Livie was certainly there, oohing and aahing with the rest of us. The excitement in the town was fierce.

Mr and Mrs Gerber came a day or so later, driving up the street in the Yank's big Ford hackney car and waving at everyone from the back seat like royalty out of one of the newsreel pictures in the cinema.

In the short time I was to know him, Mr Gerber hardly ever opened his mouth. He had a strange way of smiling, which didn't look like smiling at all because he never showed any teeth. A sort of gummy class of a smile. He was a walking skeleton of a man with a bald head and big, black, bushy eyebrows. His face was as yellow as creamery butter and the first thing he did every time he appeared was to find some place to sit down, a chair or a windowsill, any sort of a seat at all that was handy would do, as if he couldn't trust himself to stand up.

Mrs Gerber was the opposite, at least at the start, full of bright smiles, a stout woman with curly faded hair and shining eyes. She didn't just move as much as push and shove her way around. She'd even give Mr Gerber the odd shove to get him moving, all the time smiling cheerfully at anyone in the vicinity.

Livie said at once that she was the nicest woman she had ever met. There was something about Mrs Gerber that I didn't like from day one. Maybe it was that smile. Even Mr Gerber's gummy grin, if that was what it was, wasn't as suspicious. Also, I didn't care for the way Livie made up to her one bit. I didn't like it any further when I discovered that Mrs Gerber was regularly handing out money to Livie, the odd half-crown here and there, and once even a ten shilling note. I couldn't understand why this was going on and Livie said to me to mind my own business. I knew enough about money to know that there always had to be some reason for it when it changed hands. Livie was all sympathy for the Gerbers.

'They had to live in a shed after the war.'

'A shed? An' what about their own house?'

'The American soldiers took all the best houses for themselves. They just put people out into the streets and moved in themselves.'

'How could that happen?'

'Because of the war, dumbbell! That's what happens when yer bet in a war. The Germans were bet by the Americans and the English. They were left with only the clothes they stood up in.'

For an awful moment I was looking at Livie again in her birthday suit.

'What's up with ya?' she demanded. 'The look on ya!'

I was terrified she could see my secret bad thoughts. 'Nothing,' I said quickly, with a red face.

'Mrs Gerber said they had to manage on scraps. Wance they lived for weeks on turnips.'

I thought of that bustling, tubby figure moving around like a happy mother in the kitchen of the Butler House. They had no children, the Gerbers, but, as far as I could tell, Mrs Gerber was determined to be the mother of everyone.

'She must have been making up for it ever since, she's so fat,' I said, meaning the starvation and her appearance now. I gave a snort that was half a nervous laugh.

'God, you're a meanie and no mistake, Andrew. Of all the nerve, talkin' like that! You should be ashamed of yerself, young lad, about people that were starvin'!'

'Me mother and father say the Germans did terrible things in the war.'

'They all did terrible things in the war, ya eejit ya.'

'The Germans was worse.'

'What way worse?'

'They burned up people, so they did.'

'How?'

'In ovens. Me father said so.'

'Ovens? Like below in the bakery?'

'Yeah.'

'Sure you couldn't fit a chicken in wan of those things.'

I couldn't answer this one, so I had to think for a few seconds. Then something came into my head from a near lost nightmare.

'They built ovens as big as houses. That's what they did. Them Germans. And burned! And burned!'

'God, you're a quare hawk, Andrew, and no mistake, do you know that?' She turned on her heel and went off doing something else. I said nothing more on the subject but just kept mum.

The first day Livie brought me to visit the Gerbers, we were received at the front door by Mrs Gerber herself, waving and with a smile that would light up the parish.

'Welcome! Welcome!' she cried in her strange, rough voice. She wore a smart grey suit with buttons all down the front. 'Enter!' she cried. 'Enter our home.' On the top step she threw her arms around Livie and then, to my horror, she did the same to me. I felt my feet lift off the ground and was then enveloped in a mixture of muscle and strong cloth that scraped my face, my glasses falling. Waves of perfume flew over me so that I almost lost my senses. She planted me back down on the ground again, saying, 'Good good good.' She took my left earlobe between finger and thumb and gave it a sharp tweak with that awful smile beaming into me. She hurt my ear. 'Who is this little man, the friend of our Livie?'

At this point it turned out that Mrs Gerber had a job for Livie. She was to turn around and go down the town to the shop on her bike for messages. Mrs Gerber didn't call them messages. She called them 'supplies' but that was what they were, messages. I saw her handing several pound notes to Livie and a list for the shopping out of a big handbag with metal straps on it.

Livie was in her element at this job, all full of importance in the way that I hated. I thought it brought out the worst in her, attention like this. It was awful. I was left on my own with the two Germans. I think I may have said something about going with Livie on my bike but no one paid the least bit of heed to me.

Mrs Gerber brought me into the big front room of Butler House. I was never in such a big room before in all my life, so I tried to stand as near as I could to the door in case there was a chance to escape. Mrs Gerber was having none of this and she propelled me into the centre of the room. The place was full of furniture and pictures on the walls, some of ancient times, some of battles, and there were two of old people standing stiffly together, looking out at you, as if daring you to say something back to them.

Talking of stiffness, Mr Gerber sat at the end of a long sofa. He was wearing a sort of small jacket like a waistcoat but it wasn't a waistcoat because it had arms. Twirls of coloured stalks were painted down the front of this jacket and along the arms so that he looked like something out of the circus. He wore green corduroy trousers so big that they seemed to be held up under his thin shoulders instead of around his waist. He was sunken down on the sofa and looking towards me with his gummy grin.

A strange thing happened then. Mrs Gerber was standing a few feet away from Mr Gerber, her shining smile in place. Both of them never took their eyes off me, never looked at one another, as if I were a visitor from the moon. I looked down at my feet. My socks had come down around the old sandals and I wondered if I had brought in mud. Then they started talking in German. Even then, they never once looked at one another. Instead, their eyes were on me. He said something. She said something. She said something else. He said something else. Sometimes I thought there might be questions and answers but it was all rigmarole and the only thing I was sure of was that it was all about me. I was in the line of fire.

I said, 'I hafta go home now,' but it came out of me as a whisper and it made no difference at all to the tit for tat between the two of them in their own lingo.

I said, much more loudly, in a kind of squawk, 'I hafta to go home now!'

Mrs Gerber immediately came to me and this time took both my earlobes in her strong fingers. She bent her face into mine, nodding vigorously, 'Of course, little man, of course, you must go home. Certainly.' All the time shaking me by the ears. 'You do not be afraid, little man.'

Her face up close had this kind of white paste on it like a mask. I saw that there were even cracks here and there in the paste, around her eyes and around her neck. Her eyes up close had these black circles under them and there was no longer any smile. She had bright red lipstick. I suddenly thought that she looked very, very sad. This made me feel even more uncomfortable in the room because I was now completely confused by this new, sad Mrs Gerber. I felt sorry for her, so sorry, but I didn't know why.

'We are good people,' the painted Mrs Gerber was saying, nodding vigorously again, 'good people. You must not feel afraid, little man.'

I nodded, too, just to keep things going, but why was she saying all this stuff to me? Maybe she knew that I didn't like her and Mr Gerber, even though I felt sorry for her this minute? Maybe Livie had been blabbing about some of the things I had been saying about them? I wanted to say to Mrs Gerber that it was all right, that I didn't hold anything against her, that I truly felt sorry for her feeling so sad like that but I couldn't find anything to say to her that mightn't make things worse, so I mumbled again, 'I hafta go home.'

'Certainly,' she said, 'home. Go home, little man.'

She turned me around and gave me a little push towards the door. At that point I noticed that Mr Gerber had disappeared. Not a sign of him. I had never noticed him leaving the room. He might as well have flown up the chimney. I had to stand on tiptoes to reach the big bolt on the front door but I got it open and escaped. I felt eyes boring into my back as I walked down the avenue but I never looked back. I didn't go back there again with Livie until the day of the killing of the goose.

That started with Livie announcing that the Gerbers were giving a big party for all the bigwigs in the town and beyond. My father's boss, the solicitor, and the wife would be there. Dr Whelan and his wife. Miss Simmonds, the Protestant lady who lived in the Lodge. The local Fianna Fáil Councillor who was the auctioneer and had sold the Butler House to the Gerbers in the first place would be there as well. I asked Livie why his wife wasn't invited and Livie said she 'wouldn't be up to it', whatever that meant. Canon Dooley the PP was going but not, I noticed, any of the curates. There was even talk that old Colonel Butler, who used to live in the house before it was sold, was going to come back from the nursing home in Thomastown for the occasion, but he never made it either. Other posh people were coming, too, Livie said, from near and far, but we didn't know who they were. Livie said everyone was friends of the Germans now but I knew this wasn't the case, no siree! Lots of people in the town had their number.

The big news was that Livie was going to help serve the dishes. 'I have to wear a white apron,' she said, 'and a white band in me hair.' She said she was part of 'the team'. I said, 'What d'ya mean, team?' She said there would be others serving as well and, sure enough, on the appointed night a man with a dickie bow, a cook and two other women in uniform arrived at the house from the hotel in Kilkenny to work on the grub. Livie said that if I behaved myself, I'd get to see the preparations for the feast. I wasn't thrilled about going near the place again but I was dying to see these preparations.

Mrs Gerber was back in her good humour once more, not a sign of the sadness of the last time I was in the house. This was a mystery to me as I watched her supervising everything in the big kitchen and around the larders and scullery of the house. She called out orders and words of encouragement to Livie and the Murphys, Josie and her slow daughter Treasa, who had been taken on as helpers. How could people just forget bad things so easily, like the war, and go on as if all that destruction had never happened? I felt I could never do this. I'd always be carrying around the bad stuff from the past.

Not Mrs Gerber. She shone with excitement and pleasure and commanded the display of food laid out on the tables and counters, piles of vegetables and green leaves, hams and sides of beef, loaves and cans of different stuff and, above all, the special German sausages, which weren't like sausages at all but big brown rolls as thick as a man's arm.

At one end of a counter a strange tin bucket thing was clamped onto the edge. The bottom of the bucket narrowed to a funnel and a white enamel basin was on the ground beneath the mouth of the funnel. Nearby was a line of eight knives on a white cloth (I counted them) laid out like in the butcher's shop.

The goose was on its side on the floor of the cold pantry. Its legs were tied and it was wearing a sort of laced corset, keeping its dangerous wings under control. I had never seen anything like this before. I said to Livie wasn't it a great contraption to hold a goose and save you from getting walloped by the wings? She said the Germans had a way of 'doing everything right'. The goose's snake neck and head were free, however, and it swayed from side to side, hissing in rage and fear at anyone who came by.

Mrs Gerber didn't waste any time. She took the goose by the legs, holding it out from her with the rest of us scattering and screeching. Before the creature knew what was happening, Mrs Gerber stuck it into the tin bucket on the counter in the kitchen, feet up in the air and the long neck and raging head down the funnel above the enamel basin.

Then, after a moment's inspection, Mrs Gerber carefully chose one of the knives. It was more like a needle than a knife, long and thin with double blades. The goose coiled its neck, darting and hissing this way and that but its days were numbered. With one move of her left hand, faster than any goose, Mrs Gerber grabbed the bird's head, those powerful fingers squeezing so that the mouth snapped open. For a second I could see the terror in the eyes of the bird. But Mrs Gerber in the one same move had shot the knife in her right hand into the bird's mouth and through the roof into the head. When she withdrew the knife and let the head drop, the hiss from the bird was now more like the sound of a deflating balloon. Mrs Gerber went off and carefully washed and dried her knife.

Back she came again, replacing the knife in the line of knives. Then she picked up a second knife. This one was different again – a wicked-looking cutting blade with an ivory handle. She tapped the hanging head of the bird and appeared satisfied. She pulled the head down and quickly cut the throat. A stream of blood shot down into the basin, making a pee sound. The blood flowed for a little time, getting slower and slower. Mrs Gerber was crouched, watching all this intently, the bloodied knife still in her hand, the other hand on one of her bended knees. She was like a big, crouched animal, though what animal I couldn't say.

I saw Livie beside her in an imitation crouch, her hands too on her knees like Mrs Gerber. It was as if she was trying hard to be her. The blood was still flowing, all four women watching intently. I thought I was going to be sick. I rushed out through the scullery into the open air and stood a few minutes breathing in and out. I had seen enough. I went home.

Something went wrong at the big party. It may not have been a fiasco but Livie was in a state the next day. When I asked her what had happened, she just said, 'Some people don't know how to behave so they don't.'

I asked, 'How so?'

Then she said there was this big argument around the table about the war. I asked her what did Mr and Mrs Gerber say to all that? Nuthin', she said. They just sat there with their heads bowed.

'Mrs Gerber doesn't like me anymore.'

'Why d'ya say that?'

''Cause. She tauld me not to come back to the house again for a while.'

I was thrilled to hear this. Maybe Livie and I could get back to the way we were before the Germans came. I could hardly contain my excitement at the prospect but I bit my tongue.

'I just know it for fact. She doesn't like me anymore. I just know the way she looks at me, like. I'm going to kill meself so I am.' She sighed. When she first said something like this to me,

I was very frightened. Not anymore. Now I could take it or leave it, knowing her exaggerations.

'I'll still stick up for ya, Livie.'

'I know that, Andy. I know ya'll still stick up for me. I know that full well. It don't cut mustard, though, does it now, with Mrs Gerber hatin' me the way she does? 'Sides, why did ya run away from the house the other day?'

'I can't stand the sight of blood, so I can't.'

''Twas only a goose.'

'Goose or no goose, it makes no difference. The sight of blood makes me want to vomit.'

'Mrs Gerber said you have to grow up and be a man.'

'What does she know about anything, that wan?' I was raging mad that Mrs Gerber was saying such things about me behind my back.

'That woman, Andy, was the centre of my universe. I was goin' to go places with that woman, so I was. Didn't know that, did ya, Mister Smartypants? I'm goin' to take you places, Livie, on the big steamer, that's what she said, Mrs Gerber, only the other day. Africa, maybe. Who knows? The sky's the limit. She was goin' to show me the whole wide world! And now, what's left? Nuthin'! The curtain has come down on me life with a vengeance.'

'Ya still have me, Livie.'

'I know I have you, Andy. I 'preciate that, I really do, I do. Don't get me wrong. 'Tis only that I feel me whole life has come to an end.'

I thought that she might be going a bit too far with all her sighing and lamenting over her troubles but I didn't say it. She didn't stop. There were even tears and wiping of the eyes in the middle of all the frantic talk about her troubles and sometimes she'd glance away sideways over my shoulder as if there was someone else listening instead of just me.

Instead of stopping her, all this made Livie even more determined to keep track of the Germans. Someone told her that

German visitors, men and women, were coming to the Butler House to visit the Gerbers and she couldn't contain herself with excitement. I tried to distract her but to no avail. I could do nothing to prevent that last terrible encounter with the Germans. She came up with the crazy idea that we were going to spy on them, just like in the pictures.

That night we approached the Butler House from the side wall like two criminals. She even suggested we should blacken our faces but I drew the line at that and said what would people think of us. She showed me the holes in the wall where you could put your toes and the overhanging stone you could pull yourself up with and, finally, the old shed on the other side you could jump down to and reach the ground. It was only later that I realized that all this meant that this wasn't the first time that Livie had climbed that wall. She had spied on the Germans before. The nerve of her! Anyway, it may not have been the first time she had climbed that wall, but it was to be the last.

I knew right away that what we were doing was not only wrong, it was dangerous. But how could I let her down no matter how I trembled with fear in the darkness?

There were several strange cars in the driveway before the house. One or two windows showed a dim light but the Butler House was mostly in darkness. Livie had a target, a large old tree near a side window. I tried to keep up with her as she went up the tree like a squirrel. Even down below her on the tree, I could still see into the window. The room, I remembered, was the one that Mrs Gerber called 'the library', although there were hardly any books in it. There were men in there with a boy but no Mrs Gerber or any other woman, for that matter, although they must have been somewhere else in the house. One of the men was Mr Gerber, shrunken in a corner. One was an old man with a big moustache and glasses. The other man was tall and pale with a pointy face and he was the one doing the talking. The boy was looking intently at him, taking in what he had to say.

Suddenly there was a scraping of chairs. The old man, the tall man and the boy stood up quickly, looking at Mr Gerber, who was struggling. They waited as he got to his feet like a man trying desperately to climb a rope. When he was up, the thin man said something and he and the old man and the boy shot up their arms in the German salute. We had seen this salute many times in war pictures in the cinema, soldiers in uniform setting off to do damage on someone, mostly, but this was the real thing. Mr Gerber slowly raised his arm with the others and it seemed like the effort caused him great pain.

I knew then that I had to get out of there pronto before they caught us. 'Livie!' I cried, 'I'm going.' I was on the ground and scooting off to the old shed before I realized that she hadn't followed me. 'Livie!' I called back, 'Livie!' At the same time I was still moving, moving away from her, away from the house and away from that scene in the room.

Suddenly, two huge grey dogs came bounding around the side of the house. They leaped at the tree and on their hind legs almost reached Livie. One of them was dancing, reaching higher and higher. I said her name again but to myself. A door opened and the men and the boy stood there, Mr Gerber at the back, looking nervously over the head of the boy. Surprisingly, it was the old man who commanded the dogs. They shrank away at his commands, slinking back around the side of the house to where they had come from, their tails between their legs.

The tall man called to Livie. 'Come,' he said, 'come,' just the one word ringing out clearly in the night air. She hesitated but then climbed down to the ground. I wanted to shout to her but couldn't. The thin man put out his hand towards her, the palm up, the fingers bending into the palm, once, twice. 'Come,' he said again, sharply, and she walked into the house with them. The door closed.

I was never to see Livie again. I was never to see the German strangers again, either. When I went looking for Livie, I was stone-walled with all sorts of made-up stories. She was gone to Dublin.

She was put into a home with the nuns. She was taken away in a car by strangers.

My two sisters said her father had arranged for her to go to England and that she was 'good riddance'. I wept then. On the top of the narrow stairs in our house I howled with grief with the two sisters listening and whispering down in the kitchen.

My mother came to me. She said nothing to me at first, just held me close. I bawled into her old green cardigan, my glasses in my fist down by my right-hand side. After a long while she tried to console me with words but even her words didn't work.

The Gerbers left the way they had arrived, in the Yank's hackney car, but this time there was no waving from the back seat. When they had gone, the three lorries came back and emptied the house of its contents before setting out again for the railway station. The Butler House went into decline after that and for years was boarded up against intruders.

Later I was to hear that, yes, Livie had gone to England. Much later still I heard that she had a family and was settled. Later still, and quite by accident, I was given an address for her in the north of England – Bradford, I think – along with a telephone number. I was no longer that little boy then.

I could not bring myself to make that telephone call. Instead, I wrote her a polite and, I think, rather pompous letter, saying that I would make the journey to visit her, if she wished. There was no answer.

Then, not too long ago, I took out the address and telephone number again and in a fit of madness I called the number. A kindly Englishman answered. I said her name, Livie, and asked if I could speak to her. I cannot remember what else I said, what version of my despair that I offered him but it went on for some time and he listened. I think I may even have boasted of some petty success in my life. When I stopped he hesitated and then said, 'Elizabeth died twenty years ago.' A great tidal wave flooded out of me then, leaving me like a washed shell.

In the act of writing this out now, the child that I was then recedes even further from me. Give the child back to me! Give him back to me! Of course I know the madness of all this. Of course. Certainly. Just a mad old man. But that changes nothing. Knowing that, I mean, doesn't make it better. I have lost the child in me. I have lost Livie.

When my mother tried to console me on the stairs in our house that day as I howled, she had said everything would be all right when I grew up. But why, I wanted to know, why couldn't Livie and I be the same again as it was before the Germans arrived? My mother said these things didn't always work out like that. We have to put up with it. 'Time will heal, Andy, you'll see,' she said, holding me away from her and looking into my face. 'Things will get better. They always do, in the end.' But they didn't. The truth, for me, was different. I have never fully recovered.

8

BANNED BOOKS

In September 1953 I arrived at University College Dublin to begin an undergraduate degree in English. I was a thin, prim, nineteen-year-old with carefully combed red hair, a long, gaunt face and, of course, those heavy glasses sliding down my nose. I carried the double burden of self-importance and deep insecurities. I really think I believed I was a genius. At the same time I was convinced that my insecurities were leaking at the cuffs of my frayed shirt-sleeves, there for all to see. On the other hand, many of the boys and girls like me arriving in Dublin at the time from rural Ireland must have felt similarly weighed down, the first generation of their families to get an opportunity of third-level education.

UCD in the early 1950s was crammed into a jumble of buildings on Earlsfort Terrace near the centre of the city and just around the corner from St Stephen's Green. A second, science campus was located near the main Government Buildings on Upper Merrion Street. Although the origins of this National University went back to the preceding century and to the Queen's Colleges, as they were then called, in Dublin, Cork and Galway, there was evidence that the new university lacked some of the gravitas of a real university. There was a student joke of the day, which claimed that two (named) professors had tossed a coin when UCD first opened, to decide which one would teach which subject since they both had qualifications in the two subjects and, therefore, felt qualified to sit in either chair.

The college did, however, take us out of our ignorance, often in unexpected ways, sometimes through the brilliance of individual teachers. It certainly had a character of its own, reflecting the poverty and narrow-mindedness of the country in the post-war years. There was, also, never any doubt about the ethos of the college. This had to do with the enmeshing of politics and religion and the power of the Catholic Church.

Like other institutions of the new Irish Free State, the National University was largely the creation of the social class that had already assumed control of the new country, forming its first government. This stratum of society was essentially middle class and fiercely conservative Roman Catholic. It had prospered in business, farming and the professions in the latter years of British governance of Ireland. In some cases families of this class had old, Catholic money, which had survived a hostile British rule going back centuries.

The other, competing, ruling class in Ireland at the turn of the century was Anglo-Irish and Protestant. The Anglo-Irish had formed the pro-consular administration of British rule in Ireland over the centuries. They had extensive roots in the Crown Civil Service, the British army and the administration of the other British colonies, such as India. In rural Ireland they were the landlords who began to lose power through various land acts at the end of the nineteenth century that gave land ownership, for the first time, to Irish country people.

What is fascinating about the early years of the new Irish state is to see the way in which power passed from this Anglo-Irish class to the new, middle class of Catholic Ireland. This coincided with a mass exodus of Anglo-Irish families from the country with the foundation of the new state. Many were burned out in the years of the War of Independence and the Civil War.

The political party of the new middle-class Irish was Cumann na Gael, later Fine Gael. Within decades, it, in turn, was to lose power to yet another new, rising force in Irish politics, a populist, republican one, represented by Fianna Fáil and its grim leader, Éamon de Valera.

The achievement of Cumann na Gael/Fine Gael in the early years of the new state had been remarkable. It laid down the constitutional structure of governing the country, steering it through civil war and the threat of anarchy, often with brutal determination. As it negotiated the transition from the old British regime to the new Irish one, it also retained a nostalgia for the trappings of empire side by side with its struggle to express the new Irishness of the independent state. Some of this nostalgia survived in the style of its more exclusive schools, as well as in features of its universities.

These social class distinctions no longer have the same meaning in Ireland today but they were still palpable in the UCD that I entered in 1953. The college was controlled by a number of powerful men, some of them priests, who embodied the Catholic ethos of Cumann na Gael with its punitive book censorship laws and puritanical, social control of the country. Behind this power structure was the figure of the Roman Catholic Archbishop of Dublin, John Charles McQuaid, who, in many respects, was the spiritual leader of the country. Later, as a graduate student, I was to have my own brush with that man.

Some of the clash of social division in the Ireland of this decade took the form of a rural/urban divide. It was difficult for working-class youngsters to achieve university education so that most of the urban students were of middle- or lower-middle-class background. Those of us from the country were given the nickname 'culchies' by the Dublin sophisticates. There is no doubt that we represented a disruptive element in the university and this sometimes took comic form.

Two men in UCD in my time represented the power structure of the university: Michael Tierney, Professor of Greek and President of the college, and Jeremiah J. Hogan, Professor of English and Registrar, who succeeded Tierney as President. I came into collision with both men as an undergraduate. The issue was banned books, and the incident had a profound effect upon my development, and my estrangement from the Catholic Church.

Tierney was unusual in this power structure because he came into it as a bright scholarship boy from a small farm in east County Galway. In other words, he, too started out as a culchie and made his own way to the top. A gruff, intimidating presence, he carried with him at all times throughout his life something of that farming background. One description of him from those days described him as 'an ignorant man who knows his stuff'. Michael Tierney retained all the manner of a culchie even in high position, but he was also an individual of complex ambiguity. For example, there is evidence that he had ambivalent feelings about book censorship, the cornerstone of Catholic social policy in the country during that period. In my own case, however, he proved to be a vigorous censor when I dared to take on the law in a paper that I read to a student society.

Jeremiah Hogan was an entirely different individual and much more typical of the Fine Gael middle class. Like Tierney, he also achieved a travelling scholarship as a young student which, in his case, took him to Oxford. In a similar way, Tierney had undertaken postgraduate studies in Paris, Berlin and Athens. Hogan returned with a sonorous version of an Oxford accent, which he clearly loved to display. By my time he had become a college administrator and his role as professor of English was reduced. His lectures on Shakespeare, for example, were careless affairs, consisting for the most part of extensive reading of the texts in that rotund accent but with little sense of the differing characters in the plays or, indeed, of any of the art in the work. He was chairman of the Censorship of Publications Appeal Board, a body introduced in 1946 to alleviate some of the worst excesses of the original censorship process. In other words, he had a significant influence in controlling the intellectual life of the country.

Sometimes the authority of these two men showed signs of stress under student behaviour. One of the liveliest figures among the undergraduates of my day was a charismatic student from the West of Ireland called Raymond Kearns, known affectionately to all and sundry as 'Bulletproof' Kearns. He was to go on to become a highly successful entrepreneur in Irish education, establishing the Institute of Education on Leeson Street, just around the corner from the old UCD buildings on Earlsfort Terrace. Bulletproof decided to run for president of the Student Representative Council. His campaign had all the razzmatazz of an American hustings. I ended up as one of his speech-writers, a role for which he was to repay me later on. Of course he was elected. He described his victory as a triumph for the culchies.

One of the more notorious student dances, or hops as they were called, was held at the Olympic Ballroom, located not too far from the college. As a challenge to this, Ray decided to have a super-hop of his own, a hop unlike anything ever seen before. Somehow he persuaded the college authorities to allow him to use the Aula Maxima, or Great Hall, of the college for the event. This is the site of the present National Concert Hall.

With his usual drive Ray pre-sold tickets for the hop to every female civil servant in Dublin, it appeared, and made this known to every male he managed to meet in the weeks before the event. He gave me and a few buddies the sole concession to sell soft drinks in the hall on the night, which we did, to spectacular profit. The result was a night of bedlam. Earlsfort Terrace, the street outside, became thronged with female civil servants waving their tickets in the air, unable to gain entrance to the already packed hall with its locked front doors. Gatecrashers appeared and I remember at one point they climbed onto the roof of the building. In those days the roof had rows of glass windows and I can still hear the crash of glass onto the dancers below from that dizzy height.

Out in the Main Hall, gardaí in uniform were being marshalled by a frightened Professor Hogan, wearing his academic gown to give him some much-needed authority. It made no difference. The glass panelling on the great front doors was smashed by the disappointed punters outside. I can't remember how it all ended but there was nothing like it ever again in my time at UCD. Ray described it all as another triumph for the culchies.

Student high jinks tended to be confined to Rag Week when the students ran through the city centre dressed in garish outfits, annoying the citizens and collecting money 'for charity'. I do, however, remember one prank during an actual lecture.

Mrs MacEntee was the wife of a government minister and her First Arts lectures in Irish were held in the large Physics Theatre. This lecture theatre had a number of distinctive features, including no windows and steeply banked rows of benches rising to the heights at the back. For some inexplicable reason there was a master light switch back there, which controlled all the lights in the big theatre. In those days rows of nuns occupied the front benches of the Physics Theatre for each lecture. A plot was made by the boyos up at the back. At a certain moment the light switch was thrown and an agile candidate had to run down to the front in the darkness, kiss a nun and be back up again before the light was switched back on. My memory is of whistles and screeches in the darkness and of Mrs MacEntee continuing her lecture without missing a beat.

The Physics Theatre was also the venue of the Literary and Historical Debating Society (the L & H) which met every Saturday night. The one meeting I remember in some detail featured two brilliant writers, the poet Patrick Kavanagh and the author-journalist Myles na gCopaleen (Brian O'Nolan/Flann O'Brien). Their fractious relationship around the pubs off Grafton Street was well known to students who hoped, I suppose, that the rows between them could fuel a good debate at the L & H. Both of the men were drunk, O'Nolan even more than Kavanagh. O'Nolan claimed he had lost his notes and proceeded to heckle Kavanagh, hilariously, as Kavanagh read carefully from a prepared script. It was the year of Kavanagh's failed court action for libel against the periodical *The Leader*. It was also a year before the author of *The Great Hunger* collapsed with lung cancer, an illness that, ironically, led to the writing of his great, later lyrics. One of the student wits of the L & H welcomed the two men, 'one noted for his Great Hunger and the other for his Great Thirst'. This was a UCD that was very different to the college promoted by Professor Tierney and Professor Hogan.

It has to be said, however, that Tierney and Hogan did make enormous contributions to the physical development of UCD, in particular in the move of the college from Earlsfort Terrace to its new site in Belfield in the then suburb of Stillorgan. This development preoccupied the university in my time: whether or not the university should be developed as a city-centre college or given a new campus in Belfield. This, in turn, was linked to the other vexed issue of the day in Irish third-level education: what to do about the future of Trinity College? The debate in newsprint and in public meetings was ferocious in its intensity, raising again, as it did, the question of the influence of the British on Irish affairs. Trinity was widely seen as a curious remnant of British influence in Ireland. At the time, Catholics were forbidden to enter the college as students unless they had special permission from Archbishop McQuaid. Trinity still enjoyed a large intake of students from Northern Ireland and the United Kingdom, so rivalry between it and UCD had a distinct political edge.

My years as an undergraduate in UCD also coincided with the IRA border campaign of the 1950s. These armed attacks along the border with Northern Ireland have to be seen alongside the debate about Trinity College as part of the unfinished business of the country's relationship with the United Kingdom. On Monday mornings, individual students were pointed out to me as figures who had spent the weekend on armed duty along the border. Much of this might have been make-believe but it gave an added edge to the discussions about Trinity College.

One should also remember that eight years before I entered UCD, in 1945, there was a serious student riot at Trinity to mark VE Day after the end of the war. Trinity students raised the Union Jack from the roof of the front building on College Green. The Irish flag was burned and a group of UCD students, with the controversial future politician Charles Haughey as one of its leaders, attempted to storm the front gate of Trinity. The gardaí suppressed the riot but not without physical injury to some of those involved.

I believe Michael Tierney considered Trinity College to be 'alien', although, for a while, he indulged the idea of an amalgamation of the two institutions, Trinity and UCD, confident, no doubt, that UCD would overwhelm Trinity in influence and wipe out the four hundred years of English traditions in the older college. In the end the two colleges went their separate ways and the overheated atmosphere of the period passed by.

I didn't realize it at the time but the country had also begun the early process of a significant transformation. The fate of the Roman Catholic Church in Ireland was at the centre of this. These years marked the high point of Catholic power in the country. After this came the decline in that power, although we had little sense as students of the extraordinary changes about to take place in the church in our lifetimes.

Nor did I realize that I myself was going through a personal transformation in which I was loosening the connection with Catholicism. I couldn't see any of this at the time because I was a fervent, even evangelical, Catholic and was to remain a practising Catholic for several more years, side by side with the development of that other, subversive, questioning individual inside me, trying to break out. My final escape from the shackles of the religion that I grew up with came only when I became a writer in the late 1950s and 1960s. For example, one of the first things I did when I arrived in UCD was to join the college branch of the Legion of Mary. It seemed the most natural thing to do, a natural progression from my days of piety in boarding school. I couldn't have chosen a better role to express my evangelical faith.

The Legion of Mary is an organization of lay Catholics dedicated to very active promotion of the Catholic religion. It was founded in Dublin by an activist, Frank Duff, who is best remembered for his vigorous and successful efforts to close down the famous brothel quarter of the city called Monto, so brilliantly recreated by Joyce in the Nighttown section of *Ulysses*. The Legion is organized around a faux Roman, military-style structure. The smallest unit, which I joined in UCD, is called a Praesidium. Larger, more senior units are given names such as Senatus and Concilium. Our Praesidium met each week for prayer and the handing out of duties for the week ahead. The centrepiece of our meeting room was a shrine to the Virgin Mary, with candles and a statue of Mary standing on a globe of the world. She is seen crushing the head of a serpent under her feet, preventing it from encircling the globe.

The weekly duty of the Legion that I remember most clearly as a student was the picket that we placed upon a Protestant organization in the centre of Dublin, which was, we were told, carrying out a proselytizing campaign against the Catholic poor of the city. We were given a bunch of typed cards and told to hand out these to the misguided souls who were frequenting this den of perfidy. I still have one of these cards and it gives a good idea of what was involved. It reads as follows:

Warning to Catholics
At the Medical Mission, 5 Chancery Place, Dublin, free medical aid is given to Catholics on condition that they attend a Religious Service forbidden by their Church. Grave danger to their salvation and no blessing awaits them here.

Non-Catholics should not be guilty of bribing Catholics to disobey the Church's teaching. Non-Catholics are guaranteed complete religious freedom under the Constitution of a country that is mainly Catholic. Is it a fair appreciation of this to undermine the Faith of Catholics?

Your co-operation in stopping these practices will be greatly appreciated.

Proselytization had a dark record in Irish history as those of us gathered in that shivering group outside the Mission would have known perfectly well. The soup kitchens of the Famine, in particular, would have come to mind where food was distributed by Protestants to the starving Catholic peasants in return for participation in Protestant religious ceremonies. 'To take the soup', or to become a 'souper', was a particularly ugly accusation in the extensive Irish vocabulary of insult. To offer medical services instead of food also had its own sinister connotation. Wasn't it well known that Protestant doctors were capable of God knows what kind of practices, particularly on Catholic women?

I can still see the faces of the poor people out of the slums as they trooped into the Mission, often with their sick children in a line. Most of them were bewildered by our protest, some were resentful, angry and threw some choice adjectives in our direction. I also remember my own confused feelings about all this, a confusion that was to become more pronounced in the years that followed. Sometime during my undergraduate years I was invited to become vice-president of the Praesidium. I declined, but I forget what excuses I made. Shortly afterwards I left the Legion.

Why is it that exposure to the arts has a radical effect upon one person and not upon another? It is true that exposure to books and theatre in my first years at UCD had a greater influence on me than the formal education of the university. The lectures in UCD were influential in quite specific ways but there was no one moment of epiphany, which turned my world upside down.

Instead, this came through the reading of books, many of them banned, together with my immersion in theatre.

The young Denis Donoghue's lectures on the later plays of Shakespeare, for instance, bridged these two areas of my life, helping to instill a scepticism in me about realism on the stage, which has lasted throughout my life. More intellectually challenging were his lectures on Gerard Manley Hopkins because there he was wrestling with his own misgivings about Hopkins's poetry. The lectures were thrilling, intellectual exercises that lifted the study of literature far beyond anything I had experienced before.

But I was also bothered at the time by the academic possession of literature, the conversion of art into a system for analysis. There were lectures and tutorials where you were aware of the constant, transformative presence of the imagination of the artist as a filter between the page and the reader. Increasingly, this presence, the mind of the artist, came to matter more and more. Even more problematical to me, given the need to pass examinations: I was having doubts about the value of literary criticism. It seemed to me that there was a level at which the imagination was beyond the reach of analysis. All one can do at this level is describe the effect of the mystery and then remain silent.

There were two other teachers at UCD who brought something of this reverence for the imagination into their teaching in very different ways because the two were utterly unalike in personality.

One was a brilliant, deeply troubled young man called John Jordan, an artist manqué if ever there was one. Jordan, like Professor Hogan, had been to Oxford, but there the comparison ended. Jordan was infused with the power of imagination. He was mystical, alcoholic and homosexual. His encounter with literature was at a level of great personal intensity and, sometimes, torment. What was also exciting to us as students was that he made no distinction between the classical canon and the latest work of living writers. He would invest the same immediacy in Sidney and Spenser as he would in the most recently published poem of Patrick Kavanagh. This was revolutionary in Hogan's department which still appeared to insist that literature ended somewhere in the Edwardian period. It also meant a great deal to those of us who were already trying to write ourselves. We felt we were being connected to tradition.

The other teacher was Roger McHugh, who shared Jordan's passionate interest in current writing. He, too, was an outsider in the UCD of our time. A committed republican, he was arrested as he left a political meeting during the war years and was interned in the Curragh Camp in County Kildare with other republicans and members of the IRA during the clampdown on the republican movement by de Valera in his attempts to preserve Irish neutrality during World War II. It says something very positive about the power structure of UCD that Roger McHugh was taken back on the staff after the war.

He taught a course on seventeenth- and eighteenth-century speculative prose that opened my eyes to the possibilities of the prose essay. Writers like Bacon and Swift spoke to one another across time through the medium of intelligence. McHugh had a personal feeling for this kind of writing and he helped us to see that prose could have some of the detailed effects of poetry.

One of the most insightful things that was ever said to me in college was a remark that McHugh made, which I didn't understand at the time. He was talking to me on the corridor about the value of this or that work in helping one's growth and maturity. He said, 'At university you have to educate yourself.' I realized later that this was connected to his own passion for contemporary writing and the importance of reading widely to find one's own path. He hated the prevailing book censorship.

So, much of this ancillary education that McHugh was talking about came from the books passed around from hand to hand. I was very lucky. My eldest brother had a friend, a customs and excise officer, appropriately enough, who seemed to have unlimited access to banned books. How he came to have these books remains a mystery but it was like having access to a magical library. This is how I came to read modern American fiction. That, and a fascination with living writers, grounded my study of literature in a reality of lived lives, something that wasn't always available to me in academic study.

Because of its location, UCD on Earlsfort Terrace had an agreeable downtown ambience. St Stephen's Green became our garden where we caught the fugitive sunshine and dawdled with girls. Central Dublin seemed incredibly small to us at the time. You couldn't walk down Grafton Street in those days without meeting someone you knew.

Numbers 85 and 86 St Stephen's Green (Newman House), around the corner from Earlsfort Terrace, were the original buildings of the old Catholic University. There was a hall for student dances, a coffee shop, together with rooms for student society meetings and, in the attic, a small theatre for the Dramatic Society. There I directed my first play for the stage, an adaptation of Steinbeck's *Of Mice and Men*. The part of the girl in the play was played by Rosaleen Linehan. She was to become a well-known actress on the Irish stage, playing, many years later, in my own version of *The Seagull* for the Irish Theatre Company, which toured the country.

We knew the connection between Newman House and Cardinal Newman as well as with Gerard Manley Hopkins. Even more important was the fact that these same rooms were the ones occupied by Joyce and his fellow students in the scenes vividly described in *A Portrait of the Artist as a Young Man*. In our mind's eye Stephen Dedalus sauntered in and out of this or that room. Here stood the Dean by this window, playing with the sash cord between his fingers and tempting the young man with the lure of a priestly vocation.

The Joyce connection was the one that we remembered at our meetings of the English Literature Society on the first floor of

Number 86. The society drew students from many faculties, the only thing they had in common between them being this passion for reading and writing. It invited writers, like Patrick Kavanagh, Mary Lavin and Benedict Kiely to come and read from their work. Kavanagh was memorable for a negative reason because, before he gave his reading, he used up most of our annual grant from the college in double brandies in Joe Dwyer's pub on Lower Leeson Street. I can still see the farming calculation in the poet's wicked eye in the pub as he figured out the maximum amount for drinks that he could prise out of our pockets.

Mary Lavin and Ben Kiely became friends of mine. What I remember of Lavin's reading was this striking woman with black hair coiled into a bun and eyes that shone like black buttons, appearing to see everything. She became a huge presence in my life through the years of this memoir and beyond.

One of my fellow students was Tom Mac Intyre and he and I pursued writers like a pair of intoxicated fans. When you dream about writing as a young man, you dream about writers. Our first foray into this fan-worship, however, ended in disaster. Tom was later to become an imaginative, experimental playwright but at this time he was more interested in the short story. This fascination with the short story explains Tom's interest in writers like Lavin, Sean O'Faolain and Frank O'Connor. One day he said to me, 'Why don't we try to meet Sean O'Faolain?' Such a thought would never have entered my head. But Mac Intyre was a brazen man on the public pay phone and within minutes we were invited to Mr O'Faolain's house in Killiney for afternoon tea.

We sat in the garden with O'Faolain and a Harvard professor called John Kelleher. I don't know what got into me — more insecurity, perhaps, maybe a fatal need to impress, even in the worst possible fashion. My carry-on had nothing to do with our host, who was extremely polite to his two interlopers throughout, even during my outburst. I attacked O'Faolain for spending so much time away from Ireland, even though I was perfectly aware of the enormous contribution that he had made to the impoverished country of his birth. It had repaid him by banning his books. The afternoon came to an end. We fled the O'Faolain garden like two criminals, with Mac Intyre's scolding words in my ear.

Much to my surprise, Tom shortly afterwards suggested a telephone call to Mary Lavin, sometime after her reading to the English Literature Society. I swore, secretly, that, this time, I would behave myself. We made the journey to Mary's home in Bective near the River Boyne in County Meath. There, beneath the Jack B. Yeats paintings, began a relationship that was to mean so much to me over succeeding decades. What was striking about that first meeting was that Mary insisted upon hearing, in detail, our own aspirations as writers, rather than talking about her own work. Going home later, Mac Intyre and I agreed that we had been made to think deeply, for the first time, about what we wanted to do with ourselves as writers.

I got to meet many other people with Mary, mostly in her mews on Ladd Lane in Georgian Dublin. Her Dublin revolved around a triangle between the mews, Bewley's Café on Grafton Street and the National Library on Kildare Street, where she did much of her work. She was a familiar figure walking between the three and many times I came across her engaged in intense conversation with someone on the footpath. Her contacts were drawn from a bewildering array of people, often individuals whom she had just met casually – shop assistants, secretaries, bus drivers – but she knew fascinating details of their lives.

In the mews I met John McGahern and Nuala O'Faolain for the first time, two other young writers whom Mary encouraged. In Nuala's case, Mary provided valuable, basic help at a critical stage of Nuala's time in college, effectively ensuring that Nuala got her degree. I met Brian Friel in the Bective house when Mary felt I needed advice on how to deal with a pushy American producer and this led to a rich friendship with Brian that lasted to his death in 2015. She also felt that it was important that I meet an older generation of Irish writers, so I met Frank O'Connor and Mervyn Wall; the latter's work was the subject of my first published essay. But I also felt that I was meeting other writers outside Ireland, not in the flesh but through Mary's vivid conversation and gossip. In this way I first heard of writers whom Mary had met like Updike, Salinger, Eudora Welty and V.S. Pritchett.

Padraic Colum also came to Mary's mews from New York, a small man in an Irish farmer's best Sunday suit with highly polished black boots as if he had just arrived in Dublin from the Irish Midlands. He talked about his wife Mary and their many conversations with Joyce. I remember asking him about his experience with his own plays in the Abbey Theatre. He said Yeats was suspicious of the new realism in rural plays coming into the theatre, written, like Colum's own plays, by a new generation of writers with their roots in peasant Ireland.

Mary also gave me books, her way of sharing her own writing and reading. She would hunt down second-hand copies of her own books in Greene's bookshop or Fred Hanna's or from the tables and hand-carts of second-hand books then on the quays of Dublin. I still have those books, as I do Ellmann's *James Joyce* with its faded inscription, *Mary*, and the date, *December 1959*.

All these books had a deep personal significance for Mary so that she was passing on part of herself with each one. I still have the copy of Tolstoy's *The Kreutzer Sonata and Other Tales* in its tattered yellow and black paper jacket in the World's Classics series. Only when I read her own novella, *The Becker Wives*, did I discover the personal connection with the Tolstoy. *The Kreutzer Sonata* is a terrifying tale of a man who has killed his wife. It is made almost intolerable in the telling because of its setting, one of those interminable train journeys across Russia, through day and night, with the listener (and the reader) a trapped, hypnotized victim of that storytelling voice. *The Becker Wives* has a similar intensity. Like Tolstoy, Lavin drives the story beyond what is usually considered to be normality and, in doing so, she creates great art.

Looking back now, I realize that Mary and her three girls, Valdi, Elizabeth and Caroline, offered me a kind of alternative home over those years at a time when I was often lost. I even went on holidays with them on hair-raising drives, with the driver carrying on multiple narratives and many asides as she swerved around corners on Irish country roads in her Triumph Herald.

Mary may have been surrounded by a barely controlled chaos in her daily life, with constant anxiety about making ends meet, but she was propelled by an extraordinary clarity that was both physical and moral. This strong-mindedness is manifested in the tragic collapse of Flora, the young wife in *The Becker Wives*. The moment is Jamesian, the James of *The Turn of the Screw*, say, where ordinariness cracks open to reveal aspects of life that are at once terrible and beyond explanation or relief.

At that time Mary's elderly mother was still living in one of the Mespil Flats across the canal from the mews. Mary could step outside at night to see if the light was on or off in the flat. This is one of the memories I will always have of her, flustered, unsure of her emotions, as she stood searching for that light in the darkness across the canal water.

Somehow, meeting living writers brought writing off the page and into the experience of daily life. For a young writer starting out, this was a heady experience. Only later in my life did I become aware of some of the paradoxes behind this contrast between the actual writer and the claims of the work, particularly the contrast between the beauty of the work and the unattractiveness, which one sometimes finds in the character of the artist. I was to live through a time of careerism and the spectacle of writers who became extremely skilful in the management of their careers in the marketplace. You wondered where the value system of the artist resided. I also became conscious of how some writers create public images of themselves, of sage or saint, say, that have little to do with their actual selves. Back with Mary Lavin and her friends there was little of this bothering paradox of the writer's identity. Everything was forgotten in the excitement of creativity.

My meetings with Ben Kiely, by contrast, were usually in a pub. I remember one such very vividly because it was the only time that I was in the presence of Brendan Behan. The pub was The White Horse on the Dublin quays, just around the corner from the office of the *Irish Press* newspaper where Ben was working at the time. My pal Gus Martin and I arrived and were directed upstairs to a small room. This room had a table and a few chairs and little else. Sitting there, working his way through small whiskeys, was Ben Kiely. The room did have a fine old fireplace, however, and on the mantelpiece, arrayed like trophies, were rows of empty stout bottles. Leaning against the mantelpiece was a very drunken Brendan Behan. My first reaction on seeing him close up was: Look how small he is!

What followed was a question-and-answer session with Ben generously responding to the questions of his two fans. It became very clear, very quickly, that Behan deeply resented this activity. Didn't we know, he yelled, that he was the only fuckin' writer around here? Why don't yis talk to me about writin'? This gave way to a contradictory roar of praise for Kiely. Didn't ye know that Kiely there wrote the whole feckin' paper round the corner? Don't yis know how important this man is to Irish writin'? Yis know fuck all, the pair of yis! Over all this came Ben's sonorous words of peace-making. Calm down, Brendan, like a good man and have another drink while you're at it.

Suddenly Behan exploded and turned on me. I should explain that the Pike Theatre production of *Waiting for Godot* was on that week at the Gate Theatre. You! Mr Behan pointed at me, You! Have ya seen the play of me auld pal Sam Beckett up at the Gate? I was terrified but I managed to nod. Well, he demanded, what did ya think of it? I gulped. I said I thought it was very … interesting. Interesting? Interesting? Mr B. demanded of the ceiling. You look like a fucker who would!

Gus and I escaped rapidly into the night.

This had nothing to do with Brendan Behan but it was around this time that I became conscious of the need to get away from Ireland. It undoubtedly had to do with the books I was reading and the writers I was meeting who often spoke of a world elsewhere. It was like breaking down walls that were hemming me in.

Each summer in the holidays many of us students went to work in England. The idea was to make money for the rest of the year but I spent my money hitch-hiking on the Continent or watching theatre in London or Stratford-upon-Avon. Over these years I saw productions that advanced my sense of theatre in ways that could simply not have happened without travel. These included the John Gielgud / Peggy Ashcroft *King Lear* and *Much Ado About Nothing* and Peter Brook's production of *Titus Andronicus* with Laurence Olivier. This was the production that had the spectacular fall on stage from on high of the showman star, leaving him dangling by the ankle on a rope, his head inches from the stage.

The first summer of my travels, in 1954, I made the night journey from the North Wall of Dublin Port, arriving up the Mersey at dawn to a rain-soaked, grimy Liverpool still showing the effects of the war. I was to meet up with two pals from college who were supposed to have found work for all three of us. No such luck. What followed was a frantic search in the rain around the English northwest, our money dwindling and with many threats of giving up and going home.

Eventually we got jobs making Blackpool Rock in a sweet factory in the famous resort. Rock was the hard length of sticky red and white candy with the ingenious lettering of Blackpool rock running through the centre. We knew the song of the English comedian George Formby with his ukulele: 'With my little stick of Blackpool Rock, along the promenade I stroll.' But we saw little enough ourselves of the great seafront of Blackpool as we worked and slaved in the sweet factory and collapsed each evening in our digs, utterly exhausted. We even progressed to manipulating the dangerous machines, winding the molten sticky material of red and white gooey stuff onto the protruding metal arms, which then whirled it into long sticks of Rock. I wasn't long there when one of my arms was hit by a metal bar and I ended up in hospital. No breakage, amazingly, but that was the end of my career as a maker of Blackpool Rock. There was another crisis meeting and my two pals announced that they were going home. They had had enough.

I was determined to get to Spain, partly because I was obsessed with the Spanish Civil War, but also because I had just finished one year of Spanish at UCD and was anxious to try out my vocabulary on the natives. So I set out on my own and hitch-hiked to Worcester. The rain lifted and I got a job as a labourer on a market garden high over the River Severn where the land, as always in my life, helped to restore my strength over a few weeks.

The old mother on the farm talked to me about the decline of England since the war. The outside world had clearly invaded her dream of England with monstrous force and corrupt behaviour. In her disturbed mind the great river was like a frontier keeping out the aliens who would come and despoil her beloved England even more. I started to try and write a play about her for she carried the weight of one of Synge's tragic women. I couldn't do it because I didn't have her speech. Instead, I bought a rucksack and small tent and left for Spain.

I hitch-hiked across Franco's Spain from San Sebastian to Madrid and Madrid to Barcelona, then home again through France. Each night on the road to Madrid I picked out a nearby village, climbed towards it from the road, and tried to set up my tent near the houses. I don't know what the villagers must have made of this burned, quixotic figure with his bad Spanish and his passion about the Spanish Civil War. Sometimes they stopped me in my efforts to put up tent poles in the iron-hard ground and gave me a bed of straw in a shed or on two chairs in a house.

The poverty of these villages was unlike anything I had seen before but the vivacity and generosity of the people were irrepressible. Once I was invited to join in a fiesta in a village. Country carts were upended in the village square to form a rough and ready round arena. To my astonishment and terror a wild bull was hunted into this ring. There followed a noisy, dangerous effort at bullfighting with a matador, dressed in a tattered matador costume, who might have been enlisted from one of the fields. I watched all this with the excited village kids from beneath the wheels of the carts. To my relief, the bull was released at the end, bloodied but still able to stagger away to cheers and waves.

Back on the road in those days there were very few cars or trucks, which was tough on the hitch-hiker. One expensive car did stop, however. As soon as I got into it I realized that a son, about my own age, had persuaded his father to stop. The father didn't like this one bit and was clearly worried about the condition of his leather car seats, given the dust and dirt on my clothes. With his swollen face and elegant suit he looked like the Generalissimo himself. The son, meanwhile, was anxious to try out his English while I struggled with my UCD Spanish.

The son and I got onto the subject of the Spanish Civil War. He was particularly surprised to hear that Irish volunteers had fought on both sides. What kind of Irishmen had fought for the Republic against General Franco? Who were they? Why did they give their lives fighting in another country for such an evil cause? As a counter-blast to this, I was happily trying to explain the evils of fascism to him.

Suddenly, the conversation, and the car, came to an abrupt halt. A muttered exchange took place between father and son. The father had braked the car in the middle of the road and he now gestured to me. Out! The car drove off, leaving me in nowhere land. I can still see the white face of the young man watching me from the passenger seat as they drove off.

The next summer, in 1955, I was a bit luckier with the work in England, splitting my time between a canning factory in, if my memory is right, Peterborough, and a lucrative few weeks as a porter in Liverpool Street Station in London, carrying passengers' luggage on a trolley to and from the trains. The tips were generous and this time I was able to travel on a student train ticket from London to Paris and Paris to Venice and Trieste. The goal was to make that long-awaited trip to Greece, first put into my head as I struggled with Greek tenses back in secondary school in St Kieran's College in Kilkenny.

I wanted to make this trip by travelling through Tito's Yugoslavia, another visit to a dictator's land. The difference to my feeling about Franco was that I had an idealistic view of Tito. I knew about his resistance to the Nazis during the war and had a left-wing scepticism about the current propaganda against him in Britain and America. This warm feeling towards the country and its leader made two images from that night journey from Trieste to Belgrade particularly shocking.

There was a small group of us, students from several different countries, gathered outside the railway station in Trieste. We had been told in a hostel to change our money here with the touts where dinars were a fraction of the cost that we would have to pay for them in Belgrade. This turned out to be true. I found myself getting on the train that night, perspiring with fear, my socks stuffed with contraband dinars.

The first frightening image was of an unusually large group of ticket-checkers coming through the darkened train in the middle of the night, accompanied by a troop of heavily armed soldiers. There was much banging of doors and clumping of heavy boots, flashlights cutting through the murk. It was like a scene from a war film back in the Gaiety Cinema in Callan, with pursuers and pursued crossing some corner of war-stricken Europe. But nothing much happened here. No one paid much attention to our student visas. No one had any interest in searching us. Our heartbeats went back to normal.

The second image was at dawn outside Ljubljana where the train came to a complete stop. Half-awake in the dawn light, I saw, outside the window, what had stopped the train. Lines of workers were laying new tracks ahead of us and to one side. What was startling to me was that these workers were women and that this was very heavy work indeed. Many of them were well advanced in age, and one, a kerchief tying up her grey hair, reminded me of my mother bending over the tub of steamy washing in the back kitchen at home in Callan.

We had to spend all the dinars in Belgrade because they were worthless outside the country. This proved to be practically impossible in a city with very few shops and with student accommodation and food that was almost free. We set out for Greece on another train with our useless dinars still in our pockets. I think I had them for years afterwards as mementos of Tito's sad country. Before leaving Belgrade we were warned not to disembark at any point because we were travelling through the high security area of Macedonia on the way to Thessaloniki and then on to Athens.

The first sight of a small number of places on this earth will remain in the memory for ever. We can never forget the experience because that first impact of the place itself is so memorable. The Acropolis of Athens is one such place. The three or four of us travelling together were fortunate to see it and the Parthenon for the first time on one of those days of clear white sunshine without a wisp of smog in the sky. The effect of the white marble in such a display of human artifice had all the sensuality of a beautiful nude body stretched out under the golden sunshine. I was reminded of the priest Father Tommy Brennan back in St Kieran's being distracted by our questioning in Greek class and telling us that, even though they were pagans, the Greeks created great works of art and had a passionate belief in beauty.

That day in Athens we sat on a bench below the Acropolis eating sandwiches, chewing olives and swigging a bottle of retsina. We were a bit flattened by it all. A boy who looked younger than we were came up to us and offered his 'sister' to us for sex. He spoke in a strange, working-class, English accent and I wondered if he had learnt the language from soldiers during the war. I thought of the old woman on the farm back in Worcestershire and her lament for the war's degenerate influences on her pristine England. Our young acquaintance displayed a remarkable vocabulary as he itemized the 'sister's' sexual skills.

I think we were all deeply embarrassed, for him as much as for ourselves. The contrast between the words of the young lad and that shrine to human idealism behind us was simply disturbing. No one could say anything, even to tell him to go away. It was like coming across the serpent in the garden.

Again I set out on my own from Athens (there were no takers when I issued invitations to the others) and hitch-hiked first to Marathon and then took a number of old buses to get to Delphi. These were two places that had a special hold upon my imagination as a result of Father Brennan's storytelling in St Kieran's and, to tell the truth, I was glad to be on my own. Marathon was much as I had imagined it to be with its burial tumulus on the plain between the mountain and the sea. I had little difficulty imagining Miltiades, the Athenian general and his band of Greeks defending the land in that famous manoeuvre of encircling wings by the shore against the superior numbers of the Persians. But I was a bit disappointed to discover, through a visiting Dutchman, that the doomed runner who ran with news of the victory to Athens may have taken a different route on that first marathon run to the one I had taken myself, hitch-hiking to and from Athens. I had hoped to cover paths taken by others in the past, to walk and run where they had walked and run. This was my way of reading history on the ground.

Delphi had something else. Coming from a land like Ireland, littered with shrines, places that carry a mystical aura about them, a hint of magic, in a well or under a mound, I was prepared for Delphi. I had this fascination with the Greek idea that this was the location of the *omphalos* or navel of the earth. It is perhaps the finest example of Greek inspiration derived from the spectacular beauty of the setting. The Temple of Apollo rises on this terrace above the valley, with Mount Parnassus nearby. This was a place of prophecy, visited by all Greeks over the centuries seeking information from the old woman soothsayer who answered the query on behalf of the god. In some cases information handed out proved to have tragic consequences, as in the example of Sophocles' Oedipus. The words of the god could turn out to be a savage joke at the expense of the human seeker.

My travels as a student were rounded off in the school year 1957–58 when I taught for a year in a Swiss school. The school was located in a small Alpine village called Bluche over the valley running through the canton of Valais. It was between Sion in the valley below and the posh resort of Crans-sur-Sierre, higher up on the mountain. I got the job through a Dublin girl who helped to run the place and it was like having a well-paid holiday. But if I thought I was escaping a puritanical background, I was only exchanging one for another, admittedly with a different language.

At one end of the village was the main school building, which housed the boys, mostly from very wealthy families from northern Italian cities such as Milan and Turin. At the other end was the girls' chalet. Most of the girls were American, some from the families of diplomats or military personnel. There were two Colombian sisters from Bogotá, clearly very wealthy, who had their own minder in tow, a stern, middle-aged woman who resided with them and even attended classes, on guard at all times. The school was the property of two Swiss brothers. They policed the boys and girls with strict rules about segregation in a manner that would have made an Irish Christian Brother or nun very proud indeed.

Looking back on it all now, I can see that travel was but one of the ways I was trying to break through the constrictions of my background. I was struggling to find life elsewhere. I couldn't describe this at the time but I could recognize the lifting of a cloud every time I moved away from Ireland. I may not have found my promised land in Switzerland, but the living was easy and the money generous. And I learned how to ski.

I came back from Switzerland with the idea in my head of establishing a summer school in Dublin, teaching the English language to continental students. This was to lead to my own encounter with the power of Archbishop McQuaid. It would also become yet another step in my release from religious control. At the time, however, I could only think of making my fortune.

My contacts in Switzerland offered help. In those days there were specialist agencies around Europe which helped students find places in language schools. I was helped by the fact that a friend of mine from Callan, Michael Hogan, a recently qualified solicitor, became equally enthused by the idea of the summer school. This was important because, unlike me, Michael had a head for business. He was also a former pupil of Glenstal Abbey, the Benedictine school. He came up with a plan of approaching the Benedictines to give us the use of their Dublin university residence, Balnagowan, off Palmerston Park, as the location of our summer school. The building would be empty in the summer with the universities closed.

The Benedictines proved to be very generous in their response. Michael took me with him to Balnagowan to meet the Abbot of Glenstal. I had some kind of medieval image in my head of what an abbot should look like, venerable and saintly. To my astonishment, I was greeted by an elegant, sophisticated young man with a strong sense of irony and wearing highly polished black shoes. Our first meeting was brief but we were quickly recalled. There was a problem, the abbot informed us. I believe there was a twinkle in his eye.

When the Benedictines had moved to Dublin, they had been informed by the archdiocese that they would be given permission to reside in the city but under one condition: they were not to engage in any educational activity in Dublin. This was a revelation to me of how the Church controlled its own clergy, particularly its own, more daring religious orders, such as the Benedictines. While the new Dublin Summer School was not exactly a Benedictine enterprise, there was some cause for caution. The archbishop would have to be consulted.

Another meeting took place with the abbot. By now, the man was clearly enjoying himself. He announced that the two directors of the summer school, Michael and myself, had been summoned to Drumcondra for interviews with the archbishop. He explained to us, with scarcely concealed hilarity, what this involved. Each of us would be interviewed individually. We would be conducted into a room with a single desk on a raised platform. The chair behind the desk would be significantly higher than the chair in front of the desk. On the otherwise empty desk-top would rest a buff, single file. This file would contain full details of each of our lives so far, from birth to yesterday, together with family background. We would rise when the archbishop entered the room and take our seats when directed to do so. At the end we would rise once more and leave only after the departure of His Grace.

I was in a state of intense excitement at this and couldn't wait for the encounter. Then we were summoned one more time to meet the abbot. It was the last time I was to meet this delightful man. He stood in his well-laundered clothes with a letter in his hand. The archbishop had decided that there was no need, after all, to proceed with the interviews. It was a huge let-down. I would have given anything to have had that interview.

The abbot would not read the complete letter, which he was holding, of the archbishop to him but he did think, ahem, that he might read one sentence from it. And he read: 'The directors of the summer school are sorely in need of direction.'

The summer school lasted one or two years only but I believe it was the first of its kind in Ireland.

Reading modern fiction was but another way of crossing swords with the world of the archbishop. There was no question but that something of the excitement in this reading had to do with the fact that many of these books were banned. Throughout my undergraduate years I supplemented my reading of the books passed on to me by my eldest brother with more books bought in shops like Foyles in London. One lesson that I learned was that nothing in life should be forbidden to the artist. The other lesson that I learned was the importance of avoiding self-censorship if I ever wanted to be a writer myself.

Back in my second year at university, 1955, I was made auditor of the English Literature Society. My main job was to ensure that we had a guest speaker at each of our weekly meetings. The other was to make sure that the small college grant to the society wasn't frittered away in the pubs, as had happened with Patrick Kavanagh. But the highlight of the year was the society's Inaugural Meeting.

The Inaugural Meeting was a formal event once a year to give the society some importance. It allowed everyone to dress up in rented dress suits and formal frocks. The auditor was expected to write, and read in public a paper on a literary topic before a group of guest speakers and a chairman of the meeting. I decided to read a paper on American fiction and it truly never occurred to me that I was about to cause trouble. The paper was called 'The Angry Cloth', a phrase taken from Whitman. It actually refers to the flag of the Civil War but I thought it also caught something of the transgressive energy of American prose fiction of the Deep South. The centre of the paper had to do with William Faulkner and Thomas Wolfe, but I also had something to say about two remarkable women writers, Katherine Anne Porter and Carson McCullers.

Who were the guests we were going to get to sit on the panel and speak to the paper? I immediately wrote off letters to a number of English writers, trying to persuade them to come to our meeting. I knew perfectly well that there was little chance of getting any of them but I had hopes that I might get a letter back from one or two of them. Sure enough, I got a note from Graham Greene saying that he'd be delighted to have a drink with me in a Dublin pub but that he just couldn't face speaking in public. I heard from an irascible J. B. Priestley, who announced that he hadn't the slightest intention of attending my meeting and that, furthermore, he knew far more about American fiction than I did. A weird note from Harriet Waugh said that there wasn't any hope of recovery for her father Evelyn Waugh, although his serious medical condition was never specified. Mr Waugh was to live for a further eleven years and I have often wondered if he wrote that letter himself.

We were determined to have at least one live American speaker at our meeting. I wrote to the American Embassy enquiring if there were any American writers visiting Europe, on the Fulbright programme for travelling artists and scholars perhaps, who might be willing to come to Dublin. To our astonishment (and anxiety) the ambassador himself, one William Howard Taft III, wrote back saying he would be delighted to speak. Normally Professor Hogan took the chair at these meetings, not a prospect that was appealing to me since I knew about his role on the Censorship of Publications Appeal Board. But when the president of the college, Michael Tierney, was told about the impending visit of the ambassador, he decided that he would chair the meeting himself.

The meeting was, to put it delicately, tense. I can't remember a word of the contribution of the ambassador. The three other speakers, the college lecturer Denis Donoghue, the novelist Ben Kiely and the English poet Donald Davie, who was visiting Trinity College during that term, were informed, intelligent and supportive of me.

I remember clearly the contribution of Michael Tierney. He lambasted the auditor for daring to talk about such banned books in a public meeting of the college. He appealed to everyone present to return to reading the classics, which offered decent, clean literature. I knew enough about Ovid from my Latin lectures to wonder what Professor Tierney was talking about. He went even further, however, attacking junior lecturers in the college, like Donoghue, for introducing 'evil literature' into the place. Professor Hogan was silent. He didn't defend his junior lecturer Denis Donoghue and he just glared at me.

My mother and father came from Callan for the Inaugural Meeting. I remember my uneasiness meeting them after the Tierney tirade. Not for the last time, I was to experience their lack of concern about dubious public reception of my work. My father was more concerned with trying to work out if Michael Tierney, coming from east Galway, was a distant cousin of his. My mother wanted to ask about the girls in the English Literature Society who were wearing the nice frocks. What were their names? I think she was trying to engage in match-making on my behalf. Not a word from either of them about my reading of banned books.

9

THE JEWISH SCHOOL AND THE DEEP SOUTH

I remembered a Yankee friend saying to me: 'Southerners and Jews, you're exactly alike, you're so damned special.'
'Yes,' I said, 'we're both persecuted minorities.'
I had said it for a joke.
But had I?

Robert Penn Warren, *Segregation* (1956)

To learn about two very different things – a geographical place, like the American South, or a complex culture, like Judaism, from first reading about them in fiction – is to experience a benign distortion. I first learned about the American South and the culture of Judaism at the same time in my life by reading novels. I would not have had it otherwise. When I met the physical reality, the actuality of the American region or the reality of the Dublin Jewish community, I came to appreciate the appeal of that distortion and how it had affected my lived experience.

Maybe there was more of a reality to my experience because my actual encounters with the Dublin Jewish community and my first journey to the United States came close upon my reading about them and everything happened in a short space of time, between 1959 and 1965. The book became confused in my mind with the reality behind it. The most startling fusion of this kind happened when I met the American writer Flannery O'Connor at her home in Milledgeville, Georgia, in 1963. The book and the writer then became one.

Back in 1959 I was twenty-five years of age with a master's degree and a qualification in teaching. I was still living in the family flat on Upper Leeson Street in Dublin. My eldest sister took me aside and gently suggested that I should get a job and contribute to the expense of running the flat. I asked her 'How?' and she said I could start by looking at ads on the back page of *The Irish Times*. In this way I became a part-time tutor and spent one glorious spring tutoring two sons of the Mullion family in County Kildare.

Mr Mullion was a Hong Kong shipping magnate and he and his wife had recently bought the Ardenode stud farm in Ballymore Eustace. Mrs Mullion looked like a film star and was also a highly successful horse breeder. The two boys, Roddy and Stuart, were in between schools and I was asked to teach them whatever I could. This turned out to be an exercise in introducing them to the country in which they were now living, through the reading of literature and history. The Mullions lodged me in style in the nearby Osberstown House Hotel. Each morning the Asian driver arrived in the Jaguar and deposited the two boys into my care. It was a lot of fun. It was also as far removed from my usual work as it could possibly be.

Each Wednesday and Saturday we went to the races. Not only did I experience the elegant life of the Mullion family, I also experienced the race-going routine of a leading owner. I was, in more senses than one, in the winner's enclosure. Mrs Mullion seemed to be particularly successful at the Phoenix Park racecourse in Dublin, now no longer in existence, and she regularly won its most famous race there, the Fifteen Hundred. I remember a celebration in a Dublin hotel after one of these victories when the Mullion trainer, a lively little man called Paddy Prendergast, stood on a table and sang Irish ballads, to the bemusement of Mrs Mullion. When this idyllic job came to an end, it was back once more to the ads in *The Irish Times*.

This time around I answered three ads and I can still remember how I felt the absurdity of my applying for all three posts. The first was a job as a deer-beater in the Scottish Highlands. I hadn't a clue what this might involve but I had some wild tartan images in my head. The second was for a travelling salesman for the Yardley firm of cosmetics. The third was the post of headmaster of the Jewish school in Dublin, Stratford College, which had a kindergarten, a junior and a secondary division attached, all in the one red-brick building in Rathgar. There was no response from the Scottish Highlands but a nice lady at Yardley said, firmly, that I might think again about my suitability as a cosmetics salesman. Much to my astonishment, I was called for interview for the school post.

Three people waited to interview me in the Gresham Hotel: the Chief Rabbi, Dr Isaac Cohen, the chairman of the school board, Dr Tomkin, a distinguished Dublin eye surgeon at the time, and a remarkable woman with bright red hair. This was Mrs Feldman, who was the school secretary and also one of the key figures in the Jewish community. She was a woman with a profound sense of her own Irishness (and also of her Russian background). She had worked in the Irish civil service and had some words of Irish to prove it. I was astonished for the second time when they offered me the job.

Why did they pick someone so inexperienced? I can think of a variety of reasons, including the very fact of my lack of qualification. A headmaster who didn't know what he was doing would be easily controlled and directed. These people had firm ideas about how to run their own school. Perhaps they wanted someone whom they could easily influence? Perhaps I was a stopgap appointment? The one thing I did have in my favour was that I knew something about Judaism and was very interested in the subject. It is surprising, given these auspices, how agreeable the whole experience turned out to be.

The first thing I had to do – not easy, mind you – was to win over the respect of a staff of Irish Catholic primary and secondary teachers, all far more mature than me. They were, rightly, affronted by what had been imposed upon them. Slowly we reached a meeting point and things settled down. We even went on to friendships in a number of cases.

One of the senior teachers who quickly became a friend was a kindergarten teacher called Mrs Fricker. Her husband was a well-known voice on Radio Éireann as the Irish broadcasting station was then called. She knew about my interest in theatre and, one day, talked to me about her teenage daughter. This daughter was a handful, it emerged, headstrong and wild. She had announced to her helpless parents that she was about to leave school to become an actress. I said let her do it. I said if she had that kind of passion for acting, nothing would stop her. In this way I like to think that I played a small part in furthering an acting career that reached a Hollywood Oscar for Best Supporting Actress for Brenda Fricker. Brenda and I still laugh about this when we meet at intervals in the performance of plays at the theatre.

I would not have been able to survive in Stratford College without the guiding presence of Mrs Feldman. Not only did she work hard to bring the whole staff together behind me, she was also an invaluable guide to the Jewish community and the complex culture of Judaism. One of the things she said, in the course of one of our many chats, has stayed with me as a light upon Jewish experience in the diaspora: 'Mr Kilroy,' she said, 'we know we can never become employees so we have to become employers.'

My knowledge, such as it was, of Judaism came from reading books by writers like Isaac Bashevis Singer, Isaac Babel, Bernard

Malamud and the early work of Saul Bellow. I loved the surrealism of Singer. It was dramatically liberating, a world of Yiddish folk culture with its demons and angels, its divine fools and demented mystics. It was a world where physical reality dissipated and faded as one dimension blended into another in the relentless struggle of good and evil. I was experiencing magic realism before the term was invented.

There is also a sense of tragedy in Singer and it appears again, but in the realistic mode of social fiction, in the short stories and novels of Malamud. The idea of fate in Greek tragedy as a force beyond the powers of the individual is replaced here in his work by the idea that Jewish identity itself carries the seed of tragedy. I remember being deeply moved by this idea when I encountered people in Stratford College who had experienced the Holocaust.

Nothing can ever pardon anti-Semitism and the suffering, the periodic violence, that has been inflicted upon the Jewish people throughout history. But I was also becoming aware, at this point in my life, of a troubling issue at the centre of those claims made by all three major religions, Jewish, Christian and Muslim. This is the claim of exceptionalism, the Chosen People, the Elect, the One, True Church, the tragic and immensely destructive claim at the heart of all three religions: exclusive access to a divinity. It has accounted for more suffering than any other idea in human history.

Perhaps because its theme is precisely the obsession of a Catholic with Jewish culture, Malamud's novel *The Assistant* had made a huge impression upon me before I became headmaster of Stratford College. It was like reading a symbolic and, in the end, scarifying version of my own preoccupations. The Catholic drifter and petty criminal Frank Alpine is drawn deeply into the impoverished life of the Jewish grocer, Morris Bober. At the end of the novel Alpine ends up being circumcised, both an act of initiation and of violent self-harm in those shocking, final pages. Getting to know the pupils and their families may not have had the same force as reading the novel but the reading had prepared the ground for me in the school.

The characteristic voice that Bellow created in his fiction is very different to that of the anguished figures of Malamud. It is the product of another kind of Jewish imagination. Bellow's early, restless heroes, like Augie March or Henderson on his adventures in Africa, have a swagger, an energy, that is partly a zest for action, partly a matter of narrative style. Bellow writes with such freshness that it appears he is inventing a new language, one that has never been used before. What was so personally transforming was the way he used this demotic vernacular as a vehicle for the expression of high intelligence. The work was rounded with a mixture of accurate realism and the inner life of the mind of the author.

I was to meet the man himself many years later, in Dublin. He had been on the committee of judges for the Booker Prize in 1971 when my novel *The Big Chapel* was short-listed. He was the guest speaker at an event in Trinity College Dublin and I was the chairman of the meeting. Before we went into the meeting, he asked me where the toilets were located. I pointed the way but he said, no, he wanted me to go with him. When we reached the toilet he threw up, alarmingly, telling me at the same time that he found public speaking an ordeal and that he had scribbled a few thoughts on the plane coming over to make up his speech. He then told me that he remembered my novel and that he had wanted, with John Fowles, to give me the prize but they had not prevailed. I've never had a comparable experience in a men's toilet before or since.

Jewish fiction may have prepared me for my encounters with the experience of Stratford College but could scarcely have prepared me for the European experience of some of the Jews I met there.

In the 1950s the Dublin Jewish community was much larger than it is now. This was due to the displacements of war and the movement of people from the Continent into Britain and from there to Dublin. Many of the children in the school were born outside Ireland, just as many of those who graduated from the school eventually emigrated to Israel. Some of these children had been touched by the Holocaust.

A woman, whom I will call Mrs A, was one of the parents in the school. She was a striking person who wore expensive, beautiful clothes. Her face, however, looked ravaged as by some terrible suffering. I came to know her because I was intrigued and a bit bothered by how she managed the education of her children. Everything was concentrated on her boys and I felt the daughter should be given more attention. I also felt that the boys were under considerable stress because of the additional Talmudic studies they had to undertake at the end of each school day. I was clearly poking my nose into matters that were none of my business. Mrs A did two things that effectively silenced me.

Firstly, she said, in relation to the boy's heavy workload: 'Mr Kilroy, our family has been rabbinical since the sixteenth century.' Mrs A and I exchanged many other less charged opinions on this and that and I became concerned about herself, about the amount of effort she was putting into overseeing the education of the children. I had never come across such focus and determination. I tried to reassure her that the school could be relied upon to see her wishes carried out. I told her that, perhaps, she was creating too much of a burden on herself and that it was taking a toll on her own well-being. I said more along the same lines. She was sitting opposite me with that grieving face in my cramped little office. She said nothing. Then she unbuttoned the sleeve of her beautiful silk blouse and rolled it back and there was the fading number of the camp on her arm. There was simply nothing more to be said.

The experience of the Jewish school was like my travels in my twenties. I was lifted out of the old, familiar Irish world, meeting, with different degrees of confusion, elation and anxiety, a post-war European world through its displaced people, a world where history had played itself out with great destruction and suffering. I felt the effects of Irish neutrality and protectionism, its isolation and smug self-regard. All this affected me in other ways as well. For example, I was incapable of visiting Germany on my travels and it was to be many, many years into the future before I could bring myself to make that particular journey to that particular country.

Mr Wertheimer was a prominent acquaintance in Stratford College through whom I gained access to yet another aspect of the Jewish experience: Zionism. The Jewish Agency in Jerusalem sent representatives of Israel to Jewish schools in the diaspora. Perhaps it still does? Mr Wertheimer was their representative in Dublin where he taught Modern Hebrew, and, no doubt, the political cause of Zionism and of Israel, to his Dublin pupils. He was a solid, middle-aged man with a gutsy sense of humour. He was also a sabra; in other words, a Jew born in Palestine. The word refers to a prickly plant, like a cactus, and captures the flinty, tough character of the 'New Jew' of Israel.

Mr Wertheimer was a former paratrooper and there was an echo of the barrack square in his voice when he marshalled the youngsters for class. I had many lively conversations with him about life in Israel and he invited me to visit there. He said he would show me around. I very much regret that I never made that trip.

He told me that he was a veteran of the Suez campaign. I, in turn, told him of the excitement of some of my fellow students as they followed accounts of the battles in that war. The young Israeli pilots in particular, with their long side locks and yarmulkes, their prayers before diving in their Mirage jets were, apparently, a source of great fascination to young men and women alike in UCD. This was a time when Israel was still seen as a heroic little country surrounded by hordes of enemies ready to wipe it out. I often think of that today, with Israel's more ambiguous reputation in the wider world.

I asked Mr Wertheimer what the main effect of the Suez campaign was on Israel. It was, after all, a triumph of ingenuity over mass force. Mr Wertheimer replied with a guffaw and a joke. He said the war had ruined the shoe industry. I asked him what he meant. He said the Arabs threw off their shoes in the desert. And ran. The resultant supply of shoes left behind put a great strain upon the native Israeli shoe industry! Through Mr Wertheimer I was to become aware of some of the stresses between the diaspora and the State of Israel. He himself was not a man to shirk criticism of any Jews who didn't measure up to the ideals of the new state.

I was once at a school board meeting when Mr Wertheimer and the board became locked in conflict. There were two aspects to my presence. Firstly, I failed to catch the full nuances of the arguments, some of which were carried out in Hebrew or maybe Yiddish. There were heated accusations of importing 'oriental' and alien ideas into the settled Jewish community of Dublin, thereby causing problems for those Jews who wished to integrate into the Irish state. Mr Wertheimer would have none of this. It was the duty of each Jew to emigrate to Israel. Anything less was a diminution of Jewish identity.

The second fact about my presence in the boardroom was that everyone else appeared to forget that I was there. Suddenly I was like a fly on the wall, listening to a row that was none of my business. It's not the only time this has happened to me. Perhaps there is something in my make-up that makes me invisible at certain points, a capacity of great value to someone who wishes to write fiction. Being there while not being there is one way of describing the personality of a writer.

So, there I was, with Dr Tomkin, Mrs Feldman and members of the settled Dublin community as they tried, red-faced, to cope with the accusations of Mr Wertheimer that they were betraying Judaism by not emigrating at once to Israel. They, in response, were drawing upon the highly civilized nature of their Jewish identity as loyal citizens of Ireland, a gentile and very Catholic state. I have often thought, in more recent times, of those heated arguments back and forth in the boardroom of the school on what it means to be a Jew. As anti-Semitism and Islamic extremism sweep across the Middle East that issue has become a matter of life and death once again, with Mr Wertheimer's Israel at the centre of the matter.

Before I joined the staff at Stratford College I had already been in contact with the University of Notre Dame about going out there as a visiting lecturer. With their Irish-Catholic connections, they were very interested in my coming to the college to design and introduce a course on what was then called Anglo-Irish Literature. In effect, I had joined Stratford College knowing that I may have had already a commitment elsewhere. When I explained this to Mrs Feldman and Dr Tomkin, they were most considerate.

And so I found myself, in the autumn of 1962, leaving for South Bend, Indiana, with a promise to return to Stratford College at the end of the academic year. Like all visa holders to the States at the time, I carried a large brown envelope under my arm, containing a chest X-ray, which confirmed that I didn't have tuberculosis.

Notre Dame reminded me of St Kieran's College, my old boarding school back in Kilkenny. At the time it was more like a Catholic boarding school than a university. This partly had to do with its location in South Bend, a miserable place, utterly without appeal of any kind, except for its proximity to Chicago. It certainly had to do with the administration of the college by the Holy Cross Fathers. Notre Dame University is now co-educational but in my day the women students were securely locked away in a nearby sister campus, St Mary's, the college of Mary Tyrone from Eugene O'Neill's great play *Long Day's Journey into Night*.

The president of Notre Dame at the time was a famous priest called Theodore Hesburgh, a confidant of the Kennedy White House and a pal of many wealthy Irish-Americans who poured money into the place and into its famous American college football team, 'The Fighting Irish'. It was a centre of Irish-American aspirations and it took me some time to recover from this close-up experience of such ethnic aggression.

I boarded with two graduate students. This was the year of the Cuban Missile Crisis and I can still remember the real fear in our rented house as we watched the crisis develop on television with Kennedy facing off Khrushchev. There were maps on the screen showing the curved lines that marked the range of the Soviet missiles and their American targets. We were within range in South Bend. It was a strange few weeks, mixing terror with a sense of unreality. What was most striking, however, was the degree of paranoia unleashed in the country and I remember thinking how dangerous this could be if matters ever did reach breaking point. The danger is still there in present-day America.

This was to be my first experience of university teaching. In addition to my Anglo-Irish course, which began with the Irish Literary Revival and came up to current Irish poetry and drama, I was drafted into the team that taught Notre Dame's version of the 'Great Books Program'. This programme was an attempt by American universities to fill a gap in the liberal education of its students by devising a conducted reading, in the English language, of so-called Great Books of the Western Tradition, from Homer to Joyce. It had its critics, particularly because of its use of translations and the fact that some educators found the whole exercise superficial.

The version used at Notre Dame was modelled on that of Mortimer Adler at the University of Chicago. This being Notre Dame, you had, on the reading list, not only Plato, Racine and Marx but also St Augustine and the French Catholic philosopher Jacques Maritain. The teaching was in the format of small seminars and there were visiting specialists from various departments in the university who contributed more informed commentaries on the august texts, an aspect of the course that I found particularly rewarding since I was being educated myself in the process. I was learning in that most effective way of all, by trying to teach others. I was the one who was experiencing a filling of the gaps in my own reading. Despite all the superficiality and the use of translations, I was acquiring a liberal education myself. Sometimes, even today, I find myself recalling passages from Flaubert and my days with the Great Books.

The English Department had some exceptional teachers. Frank O'Malley was a guru-type teacher who had a huge effect on impressionable young men with his mixture of literature and the most recent, daring ideas of Catholic philosophy and theology. It was quite unlike any teaching of literature I had experienced in Ireland but still using the familiar ingredients of religion in what was, for me, an unfamiliar and stimulating way.

Joe Duffy was another exceptional teacher, a brilliant, tortured alcoholic who became a good friend of mine. He reminded me of John Jordan back in UCD. They both had this unusual quality as academics: they could engage the imagination of the writer at levels that usually remain hidden to conventional literary criticism. Duffy, an expert on Jane Austen, had been a favoured graduate student of Lionel Trilling at Columbia. Indeed, he brought Trilling to the Notre Dame campus while I was there to give a public lecture and to join a small group of us for a memorable conversation at the university's Morris Inn after the event. The Trilling lecture, if I remember correctly, was entitled 'The Fate of Pleasure', moving from a single idea derived from Wordsworth, then rising with that sweeping, panoptic, Trilling range to embrace Modernism.

In Trilling I was meeting another kind of Jewishness to what I had met in Stratford College: the liberal, intellectual, East Coast Jewish mind, which has contributed so much to American life. It was yet another experience of meeting the man, having first read the book. In the years before, while I was an undergraduate at UCD, Denis Donoghue had recommended that I read Trilling's *The Liberal Imagination*, one of those books that can change the way you think.

When my stint at Notre Dame came to an end in the summer of 1963, I made my first journey through the southern states of America in a dilapidated Studebaker station wagon. It was the first of two visits to the region as I was back there again, two years later, in 1965, in very different circumstances. The idea on this first visit was to go from Indiana to New Orleans, as much as possible along the Mississippi River, then back up the eastern coastline to Washington DC and then home to Ireland from New York, in steerage class, on the about-to-be-retired *Queen Mary*.

I had no conception of American distances and clearly knew nothing about second-hand cars. If I had, I would never have made the trip. I think there was something else driving me, some wild imaginative impulse that simply ignored physical difficulties. I know I was, in effect, travelling through the geography of books that I had already read: Faulkner, of course, Thomas Wolfe, Eudora Welty, but also Robert Penn Warren, Katherine Anne Porter, Carson McCullers and, most importantly of all, Flannery O'Connor. It was like trying to extend the life of the books beyond their covers. I was repossessing the books but in a new way, and finding the clash between the imagination of the writers and the actuality of lived life on the spot.

The other aspect of this adventure was the grim fact that, at this time, the South was going through a period of dangerous turbulence. In the month before I visited Jackson, Mississippi and admired its beautiful houses, Medgar Evers, the local Field Secretary of the National Association for the Advancement of Colored People (NAACP), had been shot dead behind his own home in the city by a member of the Ku Klux Klan. Two months after my trip, Martin Luther King led the great Civil Rights march on Washington and delivered his famous 'I Have a Dream' speech.

It was extraordinary that I should be in the middle of events like these without experiencing them in any direct way. I put this down, now, to my ignorance about race. There were no people of colour in the cosseted Ireland in which I grew up. I had read about the moving endurance of the black woman Dilsey in Faulkner, as well as the tragic blurring of identity of the character Joe Christmas. It was now clear that I would have to learn again about race but in a new, rawer way than reading about it in fiction, this time through collision with the untidy happenings in the streets, on the ground. Faulkner's treatment of race has its own truthfulness because, as with all great novelists, the issue is measured through the richness of characterization. But I was learning how literary art, especially poetry, aestheticizes experience, sometimes, indeed, distancing the reader from uncomfortable truths. I was now acquiring another kind of knowledge about the American South, one that was awkward, violent, untouched by the imagination.

It is possible, too, that I moved through that first trip across the South, blissfully unbothered, lost in a romantic haze. There was also the warmth of the people, which would have taken away any reservations that I might have had.

I had been told at Notre Dame that southern policemen often imposed on-the-spot fines on drivers in cars with northern number plates. My experience was the opposite. Outside New Orleans, in the Lafayette State Park, I suffered severe sunburn and later spent some time, in deep distress, driving erratically around the city streets trying to find a drugstore and skin lotion. The car was stopped by a state trooper. I was reminded of him shortly afterwards when I saw Rod Steiger in his tight uniform and gun belt in the film *In the Heat of the Night.* Back in New Orleans, images of incarceration flew through my mind. The policeman listened to my tale of woe and pointed out that my driving was a hazard to the local population. Then he told me to follow him and he would lead the car to a drugstore. He waited, hidden behind sunglasses, in his car, until I emerged with bottles of lotion, and wished me a safe drive through the South. Then he drove away with a friendly wave.

I couldn't afford to eat in Brennan's or Antoine's in New Orleans but there was wonderful Creole food at Toujades. There was no menu. You ate what was brought to the bare wooden table. Then there was the music. The highlight of this was a trio of brilliant young black dancing singers who called themselves Skeet,

Pete and Repeat. Looking back at this now, it must have been caricature of the worst kind, racial stereotyping comparable to stage Irishry. But, at the time, it seemed a playful, knowing, anarchic tap dance that was some distance away from that of Fred Astaire or Gene Kelly, which I had seen on the cinema screen back in the Callan of my youth.

My return to the South in 1965, two years later, to teach at Vanderbilt University in Nashville, Tennessee, brought my tenure at Stratford College to an end. I think I had also come to an understanding that this was not to be my job for the rest of my life. I departed from my Jewish friends with some wonderful memories and having achieved a degree of maturity in the process.

The appointment at Vanderbilt also came about because of my reading. In UCD Denis Donoghue had introduced us to the remarkable group of southern writers who came together as students and teachers at Vanderbilt University in the 1920s. They were known as the Fugitives, from the name of the magazine they published from 1922 to 1925. They were also, more revealingly, called the Agrarians. One of the most important impulses behind the movement was an attempt to celebrate the rural values of the South, the deep-rooted sense of place and the land, underscored by a suspicion of modernity and its industrialization. This was part of the shaping of the manifesto called *I'll Take My Stand*, which the group issued in 1930. The group included Allen Tate, John Crowe Ransom, Andrew Lytle, Robert Penn Warren and Donald Davidson. I never met Tate but I met the others during my stay at Vanderbilt, although Donald Davidson was the only one still on the Vanderbilt campus while I was there.

What I remember of my conversations with Davidson was the intensity of this gentle, almost frail man on subjects like race, which drove him to anger and, I think, to a kind of dead end. In a sense, I also received the message of the Agrarians from him in a pure form (although he was not the most prominent member of the group): the resistance to industry and progress, for example, the celebration of a past heroic tradition and its defeat and, above all, the centrality of religion to all this as a source of values, Christianity of a peculiarly Anglo-Catholic, High Church variety.

One of the reasons why I was so interested in this group of southern writers was that I had been struck from my first reading of them that – leaving aside the subject of race – Yeats and his Irish Literary Revival must have had an influence on them. His 'contact with the soil' as a source of inspiration is there. His discovery of a language undeadened by modernity is there. His use of classical mythology to buttress local tradition is there. So, too, is the importance of place. I was to get support for this idea when I met Penn Warren in April of that year at a Faulkner conference in Oxford, Mississippi.

I had a good guide on that drive from Nashville to Oxford for the conference and during my weekend in Faulkner country. Dan Young, my guide, a professor at Vanderbilt, was one of the leading Faulkner scholars of the day, a big, generous Mississippian and a great talker. The drive, with one of his graduate assistants, was a mixture of a seminar and a lot of gossip.

On the drive I heard about the curious circumstances of the Faulkner funeral back in 1962. Faulkner had resumed drinking again. He died in an alcoholic clinic and not, as the family would have it, in the stately family home in Oxford. I also heard about the funeral of Callie, the Faulkners' black maid who was such a presence in William's life. She is the model of the enduring figure of Dilsey in *The Sound and the Fury*. Callie's funeral service took place in the front room of the Faulkner home. William Faulkner conducted the service himself.

Somewhere on the Tennessee side of the state line, Dan Young stopped the car and went into a store. He came back with a large bottle of Jack Daniels. I was told that Mississippi was a dry state. It was also a segregated state and the conference we were going to was strictly limited to whites only. I learned about all this only after the event.

If I had known about it at the time, I believe it would have affected my response to the Penn Warren lecture. His paper was entitled 'Faulkner, the South and the Negro' and I was not conscious of how brave the choice of subject matter was in the explosive atmosphere in the city and around the campus. Penn Warren, alone of the Fugitive group, had become a champion of civil rights and racial desegregation. He had written his potent little book, *Segregation*, in 1956, a form of oral history of a return journey to the South with the voices of real people talking about race. It is as much about his own struggle with his heritage as it is about the people he met on his journey. In Oxford he made a persuasive attempt to claim that Faulkner, too, had made a similar journey of personal development on the subject of race, moving from racial stereotyping towards the creation of complete human beings of colour.

The heat in the lecture theatre was intolerable. Penn Warren stood at the podium, perspiration pouring down his face. He had one glass eye from a family accident, which kept popping out with sweat. He kept popping it back in and resuming his talk. It was like something from gothic, southern fiction.

When I met him afterwards, and he heard I was Irish, he immediately started to talk about Yeats. He didn't really want to talk about the Fugitives and I had the sense that he had left that portion of his life well behind him. Instead, with that glare and that dead eye, he asked what people of my generation in Ireland thought about Yeats.

I tried to talk about Yeats the Anglo-Irishman and how Anglo-Irish culture often bewildered the Irish of Catholic background. The more nationalistic of them thought the Anglo-Irish weren't Irish at all. 'Are they more comfortable with Joyce?' he asked, and then laughed his own question away with the boisterous manner of a Kentucky farmer.

He pulled a notebook from his pocket and thrust it at me. 'What books should I read about the Anglo-Irish?' he demanded.

I was so shocked by the question that I could think only of Terence de Vere White's book *The Anglo-Irish*. Even as I scribbled down the title and the author's name I knew that this idiosyncratic book was hardly the cultural history that Penn Warren was looking for. I handed back the notebook to him and it almost slipped from my hand with the sweat.

Penn Warren also wanted to know what I thought of Oxford, Mississippi. I had already seen the town square in Faulkner's novels before I crossed it in actuality. Courthouse Square with the courthouse was entirely familiar to me, with its galleries around all four sides, the wrought iron railings, the scarred wooden stairs to the offices above. The statue of the Confederate soldier stood upon its column, as it does in the books. I was back again in the black comedy of the final pages of *The Sound and the Fury* when Luster turns the horse and surrey the wrong way round at the Confederate statue and the damaged figure of the pathetic Benjy goes berserk in the wagon behind him, screaming in terror until the surrey is turned back again the right way and order is restored once more. Penn Warren listened to my garbled mixture of reading and actual geography and said, simply, 'Like Joyce. And Dublin.'

There was one other occasion during my time at Vanderbilt that brought the issue of race into my limited awareness. It was yet another instance when I found myself in a situation where others seemed to have forgotten that I was there, just like that time at the board meeting in Stratford College. I became another fly on the wall.

As a foreign guest, I was invited to a meeting of the Nashville Shakespeare Club. This turned out to be a get-together of distinguished older gentlemen who met at different members' homes for dinner and to read a Shakespeare play together after the brandy. These were professional men, doctors and lawyers and the like, with one or two academics, who were keeping up a very southern tradition of cultural self-betterment. The play for this particular meeting was *Romeo and Juliet*. There was a certain piquancy to hearing the familiar lines of young love in rumbling, southern male voices that clearly gave the readers themselves immense personal pleasure. The house was an elegant mansion and around the magnificent dining table, behind the readers, stood a line of black waiters in black tie and formal suits.

At some point, a lawyer, who might have been a judge, began to tell an anecdote about the court that day. He stopped short and said loudly that he would go on 'when our friends have left the room'. Immediately the black waiters filed out, as at a signal. As in the boardroom at Stratford College, everybody seemed to forget that I was present. I cannot remember the details of the anecdote, because of the accents and the coded language, but they were sharing the story of some black upstart who didn't know his place and was attempting to win a battle in the one place, the court, where the odds were stacked against him. It was a stripping-off of the veneer of cultural sophistication that at the time hid so much of the deep tensions of the South. Books and poems suddenly appeared irrelevant when faced with this actual oppression of a people still in a form of captivity.

The most memorable encounter with a southern writer, the one that had the most impact on me, was that with Flannery O'Connor. It happened on that first trip through the South in April 1963 when I was teaching at Notre Dame University. I spent an extraordinary afternoon with her at Andalusia, her farmhouse in Milledgeville, Georgia. Her mother, Regina, was present and part of the setting of this encounter had to do with the contrast between the ravaged figure of the daughter, suffering from the dreadful disease lupus and the lively chatter of the mother, who had clearly been a southern belle in her day, still having the bright prettiness of a young girl about her as she danced attendance on everybody. The dynamic between the two was complex and included a kind of mocking competition on Flannery's part, although the underlying relationship was clearly a profound one.

Flannery told local anecdotes with a brilliant mimicry of voices, both black and white, and the mother was sometimes uneasy as if family secrets were being betrayed. Home-made lemonade and iced tea were served on the enclosed front porch of the farmhouse, looking out on Flannery's extraordinary assemblage of birds. Peacocks, of course, but also turkeys, geese, pheasants, ducks and bantams. It took a while to become accustomed to the peacocks because they hid in odd places in the trees, as if spying on the world. Later, they paraded on the lawns, show-offs, perhaps when they became used to outsiders.

Flannery also told stories about individual birds, giving them human characters and names so that the existence of these creatures on the farm blended with the human occupants into a single experience. As she took me around the grounds, she was draped over her metal crutches. I couldn't rid myself of the image of the crucifix.

At first she was guarded, I think because I was coming from a university campus, and I quickly learned that she had little time for most academics. However, as the talk went on about writing, she became more open, although there were some topics where the barricade went back up again. I asked her what she thought about Frank O'Connor's short stories. She looked at me with those fixed bird-like eyes and said, no, she had never read him. I had already seen the copy of the New York edition of O'Connor's stories when looking at the books on her shelves. The stories of Liam O'Flaherty were also there. She was clearly telling fibs. It was more than lying. She had this mischievous way of dealing with people, particularly when she wanted to put them off. I think she constructed a comedy in her head featuring those people around her, as a way of dealing with strangers.

Then she asked me if I had met O'Connor and I said I had and I told her about Mary Lavin and her mews on Ladd Lane in Dublin. She was now all attention and wanted to know about the people who came to visit Mary. Then, like Robert Penn Warren in

Oxford, Mississippi, and the book on the Anglo-Irish, she wanted to know which story of Lavin's should she read. I said the novella *The Becker Wives* and I think she wrote down the title.

At some point in the afternoon Flannery and I became separated from the others in the house. How did this happen? I have no idea. Maybe I was just overwhelmed by her presence because nothing seemed to happen. It was like a non-event but extremely potent. Certainly there were no exchanges of any particular wisdom. Yet the encounter was so intense that I sometimes wonder if I had simply dreamt the whole episode. I think we were silent for much of the time. I remember just sitting beside her at one point, both of us looking out of the window, looking at those birds or rather at a world that was empty but for birds.

Then something else happened, which was so bizarre but also so redolent of her own fiction that, as I write it out now, I believe again that I might have imagined it. We were standing by the staircase of the house when she showed me a written scrawl of names and dates on the wall. It looked as if paper had been peeled off the wall to reveal this strange listing. She told me that a pastor had lived in the house and had used the wall like this to record the names of the births and deaths of his parishioners. It seemed entirely appropriate that this listing of the essential events of human life should be on this wall and in this particular house, rather than anywhere else.

Flannery presented me with a small, exquisite peacock feather. I put it away carefully in my pocket. But somewhere between Milledgeville and Dublin, perhaps somewhere out over the Atlantic on the great liner, the feather disappeared. However it happened, I had lost it.

10

DUBLIN THEATRE IN THE FIFTIES AND SIXTIES

My head was filled with details of the lives of writers. It didn't really matter to me that, compared to the wonders of the writing on the page, such details often appeared pedestrian, even squalid. I was a young man in his twenties. All that mattered to me was this belief that writers were engaged in a great adventure of the imagination, one that challenged the world that I was actually living in. I wanted, desperately, to be part of that adventure.

I was also fascinated at the time with the art of the actor, how the live actor brought flesh and blood to the words of the printed play. I think I was already developing some sense of how to write for an actor, how to create space in the writing, which would allow the actor full, personal expression. Playwrighting is a form of writing unlike any other because it is deliberately incomplete. Completion comes only when the actor speaks. One way of explaining how a dramatist writes a play is through the hearing of voices. All writers hear voices. A writer of prose fiction hears a single speaking voice, the unique voice of an individual character.

Once one hears that voice one can go on indefinitely, putting that character into all kinds of different situations. Indeed, the problem may then be how to shut up that voice. But a playwright hears two voices, that of the character speaking but also the voice of the actor, the performing voice speaking the lines of that character. It is unlikely that I was able to formulate this to myself at the time but I must have had an intuitive sense of it as I wrote my first two plays.

This may be an account of my finding my place in Irish theatre across two decades but it is also an account of how an outsider became an insider. In a relatively short period of time I moved from being a spectator of theatre to membership of the Dublin theatre community. One moment, it appeared, I was sitting in the audience with everyone else, in awe of these incredibly talented people up on the stage. Next moment I met them and became part of that warm community of theatre-making.

Actually, the first professional production of a play of mine was not in theatre but on radio, in 1967. This was also to be the start of a lifelong involvement with that medium. From the beginning, I loved radio. I loved the fact that you were free to move the action across time and space. The action on radio had limitless possibilities. You could go anywhere with it. I loved the way reality could be created through sound, a door opening and closing, footsteps approaching. Or retreating. The whole box of tricks of a sound studio.

The BBC of Northern Ireland had announced a radio play competition. I was a junior lecturer in English at UCD and I had already written two unperformed stage plays. I entered the competition and won the prize with a play called *The Door*, the title of which, much to my chagrin, was changed for broadcasting by my producer to *Say Hello to Johnny*. I think he felt that my title was too severe.

The radio play was based upon an incident from my father's life when we were children. It was one of the duties of gardaí in those days to bring mentally ill people to the local asylum. My father came home from one such journey and showed his index finger to our mother and the rest of us, utterly fascinated children. The finger was white and bloodless as if crushed in a vice. His story was that the poor, terrified patient had held his finger in the back seat of the car on the way to the hospital and wouldn't let go until he was sedated. The story haunted my childhood, until I came to write the play. The bloodless finger found its place in that radio play.

The BBC prize came at a time when I had spent a great deal of effort trying, without success, to get my first two stage plays, *The O'Neill* and *The Death and Resurrection of Mr Roche*, into production. I think the publicity surrounding the BBC prize helped to send me on my way in theatre. The radio production was also my first experience of working with first-rate professional actors like Cyril Cusack and Godfrey Quigley. Altogether, this was a good preparation for entry into theatre.

I belong to a generation of playwrights who came into Irish theatre in the 1950s and 1960s. Here is a list of some of the people involved, together with their plays: John B. Keane (*Sive*, 1959), Tom Murphy (*A Whistle in the Dark*, 1961), Hugh Leonard (*Stephen D.*, 1962), Brian Friel (*Philadelphia, Here I Come!*, 1964), Eugene McCabe (*King of the Castle*, 1964), and my own play, *The Death and Resurrection of Mr Roche* (1968). Typically, there are no women writers on the list, an accurate reflection of the way women were denied self-expression as playwrights in those days. Tom Mac Intyre was of the same generation but his extraordinary experimental writing for the stage did not come until the 1980s. At this time, as I remember, he was more interested in writing short stories.

I am not trying to suggest that this group came together with a single, common purpose or even that there was a shared idea of what theatre might be. There was no manifesto, no declaration of grand intent. There was friendship. I became a friend of Tom Murphy and Eugene McCabe and a very close friend indeed of

Brian Friel. Hugh Leonard was different to the others. He was a distinctly urban writer while the rest of us came out of a rural or small-town background. He also had an acerbic personality, which made some people uncomfortable but I have to say that I greatly admired his sense of style and the commanding intelligence behind the comedy. He was a very funny writer, with great technical skills.

We did share that post-war Ireland. It was part of our imaginative landscape, when Irish neutrality gave way to the enforced reality of the 1950s, the isolation, the repressiveness, the dreariness. In retrospect, it seems to have been virtually a cashless economy, with a minimum of material needs, presided over by the ascetic figure of de Valera. Boots were repaired, often on the home last, with heavy studs and steel tips and, sometimes, sandals were worn through the winter with insoles of newspaper padding. There was a smell of containable, endurable poverty everywhere, and everyone rode the bicycle, often on huge journeys that would now be worthy of the *peloton*. And, yet, out of this dispiriting world came what is now generally acknowledged to be the first significant shift in sensibility in the Irish theatre since the early days of the Irish National Theatre – the Abbey, under the leadership of Yeats.

Yeats was a huge presence when I was reading him as a student at UCD. The poetry, obviously, was there in all its magnificence. But I was also drawn to the vast output of his writings about theatre and, specifically, what he had to say about Irish playwrights of a similar background to myself.

The theatre he established, the National Theatre of Ireland, was largely the product of a small group of Anglo-Irish writers, like Yeats himself, writers such as J.M. Synge and Lady Gregory. Their subject matter, however, was not drawn from their own background. Instead, they turned for inspiration to the ancient culture of the native Irish, now Catholic but with roots in the distant, pre-Christian past of folklore and mythology. It was a grand vision of unity, of healing the fracture between Protestant and Catholic Ireland.

In his lifetime Yeats saw the arrival of a new group of playwrights, predominantly of Catholic background, who began to shift his theatre in a new direction. The plays of Paul Vincent Carroll, T. C. Murray, Teresa Deevy and Brinsley MacNamara were naturalistic, the kind of realism that comes from close familiarity with the subject matter. Their plays, or imitations of them, came to dominate Irish theatre in the thirties, forties and fifties. These playwrights were part of our growing up. They were the plays I and my contemporaries saw as young writers; these were our models as playwrights but it soon became clear that our work was as much a reaction against them, as it was an imitation.

From the beginning Yeats disliked these plays of Catholic Ireland. He loathed the pervasive naturalism. He even devised a theory to account for their limitations. For Yeats, the playwrights of Catholic Ireland (he had in mind Padraic Colum and Edward Martyn but his words could apply equally to their successors) were 'dominated by their subject', whereas playwrights of his own, Anglo-Irish background 'stand above their subject and play with it'. When I read these words of Yeats for the first time, I thought, yes, he is saying something that I've experienced myself, a kind of burden imposed by the subject matter. I could see how repressed Ireland could inhibit a writer and that one would have to escape this grip.

The creative distancing that Yeats is claiming for the Anglo-Irish playwrights, like Synge and Lady Gregory, derives in part at least from the fact that, in writing about Catholic Ireland, the Anglo-Irish playwrights were writing about a people who were separated from them, in a profound way, politically, socially, religiously and economically. With some exceptions, like Denis Johnston and Mary Manning, the Anglo-Irish playwrights during Yeats's lifetime never really drew upon their own social background in their plays. Instead, they turned to the native Irish tradition. Synge began by trying to write about his own background but quickly turned instead to peasant Ireland where his genius achieved fruition.

The typical play of the time was what used to be called the 'peasant' play. In the work of Synge this produced glorious results. In the countless kitchen plays of social realism that followed, the results were less happy, set in a rural Irish kitchen with a number of stock characters who appeared over and over again: the long-suffering mother, the garrulous neighbours, the local teacher and local parish priest, the last two often in conflict over social issues. One unkind but accurate joke did the rounds of Dublin theatre in the sixties. It was said that the Abbey never had to change its set as each play unfolded in the same kitchen. All that was required for each production was a coat of new paint and the show could go on!

Looking back on this endless stream of rural kitchen drama one can understand Yeats's impatience. In part, his distaste for these naturalistic comedies and tragedies was a distaste for sociology or rather the sociological burden of a writer working close to the material. Art should never try to compete with journalism, otherwise it will never come into contact with mystery and what lies beyond the rational. Yeats is calling for a freedom from realism on the stage. I think, in different ways, my own generation achieved the kind of freedom proposed by Yeats. I certainly remember that my contemporaries shared this impatience of Yeats with the current, tired realism on the Irish stage at that time.

In 1987 the School of Education at Trinity College Dublin produced a remarkable report on the relationship between creativity and education in Ireland, which casts a light upon writing for the theatre when I started to write plays. The interviews of the playwrights included in this report give a vivid picture of my own generation and of how the Ireland of the forties and fifties became refracted into the imaginative life of our plays. This was often in the form of rebellion against naturalism but also against the prevailing, dominant Catholicism. Here is Tom Murphy with his friend Noel O'Donoghue, who collaborated with Murphy in the writing of his first play, *On the Outside*.

One Sunday morning we were standing in the square in Tuam after the last Mass. This was the usual thing to do, talking about football. We felt infinitely superior to the plebs. O'Donoghue said to me, 'Why don't you write a play?' I said, 'What would we write about?' And he said, 'One thing is fucking sure, it's not going to be set in a kitchen.' That was the most progressive thing anybody had ever said to me.

Life bounded by the country kitchen. Over the years Irish plays continued to be set in rural kitchens, written by Murphy as well as by other playwrights, for the very good reason that Ireland continued to act out her dramas there. That moment of rebellion on the square of Tuam, however, had its own significance. It heralded the end of the peasant play.

It took two exceptional plays, Murphy's *Bailegangaire* and Friel's *Translations* to effect this demise, to finally exhaust the form of the peasant play and put a seal upon it. I want to go outside the timeframe of this book for a moment, to indicate the historical importance of these two plays. I remember when I saw both plays for the first time, in the 1980s: they brought back memories of when we had first started out in the theatre twenty years before that, and our challenges at the time to the conventional peasant play. There is a distinct sense of an ending in both plays. Each is a theatrical elegy for the life it acts out. Each location, Murphy's 'country kitchen' and Friel's 'hay-shed or byre' is being used for a function for which it is not intended. Friel's school in a byre and Murphy's bed in the kitchen are jolting images for the audience. There is a displacement here, a dehiscence, as Beckett once memorably observed of O'Casey's farce, in which the suffering of individuals stands in for the shifting of the floor of a whole civilization.

There were two other opening nights that stood out, technically, as exemplifying the new drama back in the 1960s: Hugh Leonard's *Stephen D.* and Brian Friel's *Philadelphia, Here I Come!* These are the two productions that demonstrated the freshness and originality of the new drama. What is interesting, however, is that these two plays were not innovative in theme. Leonard was drawing upon the well-tried Joycean themes of the Irish family, religion and the struggle for identity, the very nets from which Joyce himself had escaped. Friel's play draws upon a very similar array of subjects but his primary theme is one that dominated Irish politics when he was writing the play: emigration. Leonard brought a cinematic fluidity to the dramatic narrative of the Joycean material. His treatment had a contemporary feeling to it. Although his play is set in the dreaded rural kitchen, Friel calls for a highly imaginative use of stage space that corresponds to the divided self at the centre of the play. For those of us who saw these two opening nights there was an overwhelming sense of doors opening into a future of change and freedom.

The originality was mainly technical. I think a clue to this is that both productions were driven by the genius of two gifted directors, Jim Fitzgerald of the Leonard play and Hilton Edwards of the Friel. Irish drama was not known at the time for the technical excellence of its productions. One can now see how the writing invited this directorial treatment, how both Leonard and Friel were drawing upon their experience of contemporary theatre outside Ireland and were inviting the very best technical resources of the modern stage into their productions. In effect they were bringing Irish theatre into the present day. But there were also other stirrings in Irish life at that time that contributed to this change.

The standard reading of the 1950s is of a time of stagnation, of sapping emigration, with social and economic misery at home. It is true that over 400,000 people emigrated in the decade and particularly notable was the number of young women who left. Areas of rural Ireland were devastated. There were other social problems. This is the decade that we most associate with the horrors of industrial schools and Magdalene laundries, of abused, lost children and an official indifference at the highest level to what was going on.

Like all generalizations, however, this doesn't quite capture the full complexity of the times. There were other energies in the air as well. An older Ireland and an Ireland about to be reborn came into painful collision. What was happening in Ireland was also happening elsewhere in Europe, a typical post-war process of transformation. The difference, perhaps, was in the degree of resistance to change in Ireland. This may have been due to isolationism.

There was also another energy in the artistic scene in Dublin at the time, an energy that sometimes rises up out of impoverishment. Writers like Brian Fallon, Eoin O'Brien and Adrian Frazier have written about this energy of impoverishment at the time and I experienced it myself.

Patrick Kavanagh represented this power for us when we were students, a figure of some squalor who produced exquisite poetry. We saw him stalking through the streets near St Stephen's Green with that sartorial stamp, the swinging, dirty raincoat, the dipped brooding hat, the notorious cough and splutter, arms akimbo, knotted like an embrace that had lost or crushed its love object. He was a man of high intelligence, a lover of stillness and epiphanies, a very private man who lived behind this mask of ridicule, contrariness and insult. The mask protected the delicacy of the poems and the numerous, glittering insights of the prose. Brendan Behan was another such figure out of this world of booze and desperation.

I faced this Dublin with a confused anger and a rush of writing. I wrote an essay in 1959, 'Groundwork for an Irish Theatre', published in the Jesuit magazine *Studies*, excoriating Dublin theatre for its conservatism and shabby standards, even as I enjoyed some excellent productions in the same theatre. Looking through this essay again after a gap of several decades, I am relieved that there isn't too much youthful arrogance in it. For example, it does acknowledge that Dublin theatre in the 1950s was, on the whole, admirable in its ambition. It was when I was beginning to experience first-rate professional theatre in Dublin. The energy coming off the stage was palpable, physical, but created by the imagination.

I had studied drama at UCD. Now I was experiencing drama on stage and learning about the nature of stage action, something that cannot really be conveyed through the act of reading. Going to theatre was like having an alternative, parallel education. I was giddy with the sense of possibility for myself as a writer. In my first year as a student at UCD I saw Hilton Edwards's great Gate production of *St Joan* with Siobhán McKenna. Apart from Siobhán, Hilton and Michael, it was distinguished by its cast, including an unforgettable Jack MacGowran and a very impressive Denis Brennan. There was also Edwards's production of *Othello* at the Olympia Theatre with Mac Liammóir and Maureen Cusack. This was a time, too, when try-outs for the London theatre came to Dublin, particularly to the Olympia under the Illsley-McCabe producers. In this way I saw Alec Guinness, Wilfrid Lawson and Noel Willman in a play called *The Prisoner* by Bridget Brophy. This play had its own notoriety because it was based upon the contro- versial case of Cardinal Stepinac and his imprisonment by Tito's communist regime in Yugoslavia. The cardinal's case was at the centre of Cold War politics for a period and became something of a cause in Catholic Ireland.

In fact it was possible, in the Dublin of the 1950s to see more professional productions of European and American plays, than perhaps is true of today. I saw plays by Ugo Betti, Pirandello, Genet, Jean Anouilh, Sartre, William Inge, Lillian Hellman, Arthur Miller and Tennessee Williams. This was largely due to the vision of a remarkable group of directors and producers: Alan Simpson, Jim Fitzgerald, Hilton Edwards, Phyllis Ryan and Barry Cassin and his theatrical partner, Nora Lever. These individuals ran a number of courageous companies like the Pike, the Gate, the Globe, Theatre Studio 37 and Orion and Gemini Productions.

The target of my attack in the *Studies* essay was actually the Abbey Theatre. As I tried to point out at the time, this was partly because of its status as a National Theatre and the expec- tations that accompanied this standing. 'Most Irish dramatists,'

I announced, 'dream of seeing their plays presented on the boards of the Abbey, performed by the Abbey Company.' This was very much the daydreaming of a young man who was trying to write plays himself. I also criticized the Abbey's managing director, Ernest Blythe, for rejecting plays by Brendan Behan (*The Quare Fella*), John B. Keane (*Sive*) and Tom Murphy (*A Whistle in the Dark*), plays that were highly successful when performed elsewhere.

I had also criticized Irish playwrights (although not Mr Behan) for their lack of technical daring and for shirking what I called 'the painful, sometimes tragic problems of a modern Ireland which is undergoing considerable social and ideological stress'. Gabriel Fallon, a board member of the Abbey, responded to my essay with one of his own in *Studies*, in which he advised me, that, if I was so worked up, I should go and write a play myself. I think he was surprised when I did.

At the time, most people in Irish theatre considered that the Abbey was in a rut. There was a palpable sense of boredom and frustration among the actors. But, given the right opportunity, say, playing Brecht under Tomás Mac Anna, they could reveal great power and imagination on stage. The *malaise*, compounded by alcohol and laziness, went beyond any one element of theatre and was rooted in the culture itself.

The impetus for my attack had come from outside theatrical influences that hit me during those years. One was the experience of some superb English classical acting. I saw John Gielgud's *King Lear* in London in 1955, directed by George Devine. I was very aware of the publicity surrounding Gielgud's arrest for soliciting gay sex some time before the production and of the sensible way in which the British authorities had handled the scandal. Gielgud's *Lear* was hampered by meaningless orientalism in the form of stage and costume design by Isamu Noguchi. I was, however, entranced by the whole experience. I remember going around to the stage door of the Palace Theatre, joining the queue to see the star. I brought back home Gielgud's autograph, written on the cover of the play's programme. One of my older brothers expressed shock at my close encounter with such a scandalous person. Of the two plays in the Gielgud season I was much more enamoured of the companion piece to the *Lear, Much Ado About Nothing*, in which Gielgud was partnered by Peggy Ashcroft. This Shakespearean theatre had the effect of creating standards in my mind, perhaps ideal standards that had little actual influence upon me, but standards nevertheless.

I also had two other, very different, theatrical experiences in London and they did affect my writing in a direct way. One was the new English drama of the 1950s and the other was the concurrent effect of Brecht on the anglophone theatre at this time. The key date is 1956. This was the year of my graduation from UCD and of the premiere of John Osborne's play *Look Back in Anger* at the Royal Court Theatre in London. Like everyone else who saw it, I was startled by its rage and energy. Two years later I saw Osborne on stage himself, an elegant figure as an actor, in *The Making of Moo*, a poor effort at the satire of religion by Nigel Dennis.

Nineteen fifty-six was also the year of the first visit to London from East Berlin of Brecht's company, the Berliner Ensemble. I didn't see it but I saw the effect of its staging techniques on English directors like George Devine and Joan Littlewood and on Hilton Edwards and Tomás Mac Anna back in Dublin. Stage space had suddenly become a place of exciting freedom of movement. I think that Hilton Edwards had little interest in Brechtian ideology. What must have impressed him, however, was the way in which Brecht embedded realism inside highly stylized staging, with the frontal immediacy of the productions and the direct way in which the plays addressed the audience.

I saw the influence of Brechtian staging, particularly of crowd scenes, in Mac Anna's production of Brecht's *The Life of Galileo* at the Abbey in 1956 and Edwards's production of *St Joan of the Stockyards* in 1961 with Siobhán McKenna. This was a companion piece to his earlier production of Shaw's *St Joan*, again with Siobhán. But you could also see this new epic sweep in Edwards's Shakespearean work, as in his *Julius Caesar*, in fascist costume, in 1957. So, too, I remember the movement and stage energy of Simpson's production of James McKenna's *The Scatterin'* in 1960, that rarity in Irish theatre, a local pop musical. My own writing of the history play *The O'Neill* came very much out of this particular stable of influences.

The new English drama of Osborne, Shelagh Delaney, John Arden and Arnold Wesker showed how courageous writing could tackle serious issues in the theatre. Brechtian technique, on the other hand, broadened my sense of non-verbal theatre. I was drawn to the alternative languages of the stage, other than that of words: the language of the body, the language of visual imagery, the language of silence and the empty stage.

The high point of my experience of this kind of theatre came a little later at the Odeon Theatre in Paris in a production of Flaubert's *La Tentation de Saint Antoine* by the Swiss choreographer Maurice Bejart, with Jean-Louis Barrault as the saint. This must have been before 1968 when the students ransacked the theatre and created such a crisis for Barrault. Bejart created a high ramp, like a models' catwalk, through the auditorium. Down this walkway paraded the fantastic visions of the troubled saint, like figures from Kabuki. The near-naked Barrault, meanwhile, was writhing in a sandpit on stage, projecting these visions of hell into the audience. This was a liberating theatre that eventually inspired me to write plays like *Talbot's Box* (1977) and *The Secret Fall of Constance Wilde* (1997).

It is clear that Dublin was going through something of a revolution in the art of staging and that, to some extent, this was influenced by what was going on in British theatre. The Dublin Theatre Festival, too, was crucial to all this. The history of Irish theatre in the period is inextricably bound up with the history of the festival. It is important to remember that Fitzgerald's production of Leonard's *Stephen D.* and Edwards's production of Friel's *Philadelphia, Here I Come!* were both festival productions.

The Dublin Theatre Festival began as an offshoot of An Tóstal. So, its first year, 1957, was part of the sixth year of An Tóstal. But what was An Tóstal? It was a spring festival throughout the country engineered by the staff of the Irish Tourist Board to extend the tourist season by pushing it back from summer into spring. The Irish weather consistently played havoc with this invented bacchanalia. The point is, however, that the Theatre Festival began under this particular umbrella of official Ireland with its political, social and clerical establishment. For example, the festival was launched with a celebration of the Catholic mass. In another seal of official approval, the first year started with a garden party at the Royal Marine Hotel out in Dun Laoghaire and a festival gala dinner in the Shelbourne Hotel, while the suits and frocks turned out again in the dress circle of the old Theatre Royal, now long gone, to see Margot Fonteyn and the Royal Ballet.

It was a bit like the Irish establishment of the new Irish Free State so brilliantly mocked by Denis Johnston in *The Old Lady Says 'No'!* I saw this play for the first time in its revival at the Gate in that first year of the festival in 1957. And although Mac Liammóir was clearly too old for the part of Robert Emmet, which he had first played nearly thirty years earlier, the play itself was a revelation of energetic theatricality. I loved its experimentalism. Its targets, too, of blood sacrifice and the romantic evasion of reality, seemed entirely apt for the times as the IRA campaign gathered momentum in the North and the realities of life in Ireland made romanticism irrelevant, even immoral.

I believe the actual idea of a theatre festival may have come from one man, Brendan Smith. Although born in England, Smith seemed a quintessential Dubliner, a theatre producer who ran a professional acting academy in the city. Some people looked upon him as a fuddy-duddy, conservative type. He certainly knew how to play upon the leaders of official Ireland, both lay and clerical. But I was to learn in the 1960s that he was a man of exceptional courage, a risk-taker, when he produced my play *The Death and Resurrection of Mr Roche* at the Olympia Theatre.

When he announced that first festival programme in 1957, Brendan Smith expressed regret that the one thing missing was the premiere of a new play. While he was involved, Smith struggled to make this goal central to the festival. The other plank of his artistic policy was to bring an international presence to the festival. He brought Jean Vilar's company Théâtre National Populaire from Paris that first year to perform Molière.

Smith's policy of performing new plays came more and more to the fore. Over the next decade, until my own involvement in 1968, he was responsible for new plays by Hugh Leonard, John B. Keane, Brian Friel, Eugene McCabe, James McKenna, Máiréad Ní Ghráda, M.J. Molloy, G.P. Gallivan, James Douglas and Bryan Mac Mahon. In effect, the festival became known as an outlet for new plays and people began to write plays specifically for the festival. It helped enormously that foreign critics came regularly to Dublin to review the plays. So a play that might be difficult to produce outside the festival found its place within it.

The shows that made a considerable impact upon me in that first year of the festival were Jim Fitzgerald's productions of Yeats's plays for the Globe Theatre in Dun Laoghaire and Alan Simpson's production of *The Rose Tattoo* by Tennessee Williams in the small Pike Theatre.

I already knew Fitzgerald's skilful direction for the Globe Theatre Company, with Godfrey Quigley, Pauline Delaney and Norman Rodway. I didn't see all seven Yeats plays but I saw enough to learn something about how Yeats's idea of theatre could still speak to the second half of the twentieth century. I also saw how a director with an acute sense of contemporary theatre could do something new with Yeats's plays. The whole experience of the Globe Theatre was given an added piquancy by the fact that performances took place in the theatre of the Gas Company on the main street of Dun Laoghaire. To get to your seat you had to wend your way past refrigerators, washing machines and other items of gas-powered technology.

My encounter with *The Rose Tattoo* is one of the more shameful memories of my whole life. Unlike my taking a stand in defending banned books as a student in 1955, this time around I failed to measure up to the challenge of stage censorship. I don't think I have ever completely recovered from it.

In 1957 I was already trying to write plays and I was mad about theatre. I went to Alan Simpson and asked him for any kind of job he could give me in the Pike. He put me in the box office, helping to sell tickets. The Pike had been raided by the police during the run of *The Rose Tattoo* in a clumsy attempt to prosecute the theatre for indecency. I came under extreme pressure to leave my post. Indeed, it was suggested, but not by the university, that I would be unable to continue my graduate studies if I were associated with the prosecution of the theatre in the courts. Absurd, I know, but this was typical of the atmosphere of the times.

When I talked to Alan Simpson about this, he told me to go home, which I did, along with a couple of others of the company who were under similar pressure. It didn't make it any better that, when Alan took over at the Abbey Theatre in the 1960s, he was responsible for seeing my play *The O'Neill* into production at the Peacock twelve years after my timid behaviour at the Pike. He became a good friend.

The shock was that, even though I was prepared to fight book censorship, there was still a way in which repressed Ireland could make me behave in this manner. I now think I was unable to fully free myself from the incubus of the Ireland I grew up in until I had finished writing *The Death and Resurrection of Mr Roche.* Writing that play was a way of growing up and facing the fears and guilt inculcated into me in my childhood.

I think I started to write a play about a group of men in a Dublin flat around the time of that incident at the Pike. It was based upon a story that I had heard about a number of drunken men who had brought a female prostitute back to a flat and assaulted her. In the original story, they thought they had killed her and abandoned her near the canal. I went through multiple drafts of this play but I couldn't get it right. The problem was the presence of the woman.

Then, one day (why I don't know) I changed the role of the woman to a gay man and the play wrote itself in a week. This was one of those remarkable gifts that the imagination some-times offers one, unsought, mysterious, coming from some deep well within. My friend Frank McGuinness says that this is a play about heterosexuality, not homosexuality, and I think he's right. Changing the sex of the victim from female to male concentrated the play on maleness, on the dynamic of violence and frustration in which the play is grounded. But I also think that my choice of a gay man was an important liberation of myself from the kind of forces that had led to my failure of nerve at the Pike Theatre in 1957. I remember saying something like this to Alan Simpson years afterwards. He just laughed and said, 'Well, at least it led to the writing of a play.'

In 1958 I was teaching in Switzerland, so I missed the brou-haha when the Theatre Festival was cancelled that year. A friend sent me a copy of the statement of Archbishop John Charles McQuaid with its papal cadences, announcing that, since Joyce's *Ulysses* and a play by O'Casey were to feature in the festival, he was not going to allow the usual mass to be said to mark the opening of An Tóstal. Like my own wilting at the Pike, the Council of the festival caved in, even though they had asked a reluctant O'Casey for the play in the first place. Brendan Smith tried hard to salvage the festival. An effort was made to move it from the spring to the autumn, away from the dates of An Tóstal and its official morality. This didn't work and the festival was cancelled for that year.

I truly believe that this incident strengthened rather than weak-ened the festival. The absurdity of it was so manifest that people changed in their attitude towards the arts in Ireland, becoming more liberal. One further step was taken towards the diminishment of censorship in the country. The anger it generated in the theatre was no bad thing, although it took some time before Brendan Smith was able to redevelop the international dimension of his programming once more. I suppose people outside Ireland simply didn't want to know. For a few years, then, the festival was very much a Dublin festival.

When I was struggling with *The Death and Resurrection of Mr Roche,* I turned aside from it more than once and it was as a kind of relief that I wrote *The O'Neill* in either 1963 or 1964. This is how *The O'Neill* became the first completed stage play that I wrote, although, in the end, *The Death and Resurrection of Mr Roche* was the first to be produced.

So it was that I had ended up with two plays, not just one, looking for production. The two plays started doing the rounds, two very different works in style and content. They became enmeshed, like two unhappy partners, one pulling back the other. Having both of them on offer at the same time was no help.

I sent *The O'Neill* to Hilton Edwards and received his response in a three-page letter in June 1964. He said: 'I like the play in so far as it holds the attention, is fresh in its approach with, as far as I can judge, a contemporary parallel, and it is in the main actable and would be interesting to produce. I like its freedom of form.' But then he went on to talk about the economic difficulties facing Irish theatre of the day: 'This latter point is of particular importance because the cast of your play, while by no means too big for your requirements, is larger than we can cope with in the Dublin theatre under present economic conditions – It is because I can no longer put on Shakespeare or anything but piddling little plays that I am keeping out of the scene.'

It was around this time, too, that Hilton advised me to get an agent. With his help, and her reading of *The O'Neill,* I was taken on by Peggy Ramsay. She was a London agent who had an enormous influence on English theatre of the twentieth century.

(Something of her outrageous character can be experienced in the film about Joe Orton, *Prick Up Your Ears* where she is played by Vanessa Redgrave.) Peggy was a turbulent, hugely creative presence in my own writing career until her death in 1991.

I will tell one story about Peggy, which catches something of her fiery quality. When *The Death and Resurrection of Mr Roche* had its first production, it got a rave review from Irving Wardle in *The Times*. Wardle sent the review to *The New York Times*, which reprinted it. I asked Peggy for the name of a New York agent to represent the play and she suggested Lucy Kroll, among several others. I sent the play to Lucy. Before I had drawn breath she suddenly arrived at my doorstep in Dublin, waving a letter from the producer David Merrick, offering a first-class Broadway production of the play. When Peggy heard this, she was livid. I tried to get across to her that it was her suggestion that led to the involvement of Lucy Kroll in the first place.

The truth is that I was out of my depth. My friend Mary Lavin saw my confusion. She set up a dinner in her home in County Meath with Brian Friel, who had recently had a Broadway triumph with the same David Merrick. There, for the first time, under the Jack Yeats paintings, I heard the brilliant anecdotes of Brian, the hilarious mimicry, as he took me through the shark-infested waters of New York theatre. He said the Merrick letter meant nothing (he was right, of course). Letters mean nothing in the business. All that mattered was a contract. In the end I never went anywhere with Lucy Kroll. Peggy calmed down and soon forgot all about the upheaval.

I became involved with other theatre correspondence. It is clear to me now, looking back, that I was no longer an outsider in theatre. Theatre business has a reputation for bitchery but the truth is that it is also a community of generosity, particularly towards young newcomers. I felt at the time that it was like becoming a member of an ancient guild, with the elders there, aside, waiting with advice and help.

The O'Neill went to the Abbey Theatre and I got an enthusiastic letter from the managing director, Ernest Blythe, with precisely the same comment as that of Hilton Edwards about the economics of staging the play. The Abbey was still awaiting the opening of the new theatre after the fire of 1951. There was the suggestion that *The O'Neill* might suit the new Peacock space. The date of Blythe's letter is May 1966, just two months before the opening of the new building.

Blythe also revealed that Abbey readers were divided in their response to the play but that 'some of those who heard from others a view directly contrary to their own first impressions, expressed a wish to re-read the script before coming to a final judgement'. He himself, however, admired it. Given his reputation as someone who blocked the production of new plays, I feel I need to stress the support that he gave to my play. Moreover, his enthusiasm for *The O'Neill* remained, even though he sensed that it might provoke controversy when produced: 'However, while *The O'Neill* is not a play that might be expected to be wildly popular or a money-spinner and might indeed even provoke some public anger, we think it far better than any previous play about O'Neill that has come to us. It merits serious consideration.' It took five more years before *The O'Neill* appeared on that new Peacock stage, while the production of *The Death and Resurrection of Mr Roche* came before it, in 1968.

Hilton hated the world portrayed in *Mr Roche* and, while he praised the writing, he demolished that world with typical aplomb. You can almost hear that booming voice in the words that he wrote to me on the subject: 'Maybe it's my generation but, much as I appreciate its almost photographic *verité*, it reveals a side of life that I prefer to dismiss as I would the contemplation of my natural functions.'

It is a measure of the man's great generosity that he wrote to me again, later, on that play. He told me that the opinions of others whom he respected had sent him back again to the play and that he had now reached something like respect for it.

It was a friend of mine, the actor T.P. McKenna, who took *The Death and Resurrection of Mr Roche* into the Abbey and submitted it to the management. T.P. was a member of the Abbey Acting Company. Mr Blythe rejected the play but he didn't write to me about this. This was just a year after his enthusiastic letter to me about *The O'Neill*. By this time, too, Tomás Mac Anna had come into the Abbey, although working, it has to be said, under severe restrictions imposed by Blythe. Mac Anna's title, like that of Alan Simpson after him, was Artistic Advisor, not Director, and that speaks for itself. The Abbey has always displayed a skill in its use of titles and appointments. Tomás was to become a great supporter of my work in the theatre in future years. One of the first letters he wrote to me, however, was on the rejection of *Mr Roche*:

I am returning Mr Roche as the Managing Director feels it is not our line of territory. I would add to that one word – yet. However, it does seem to me that if Jim Fitzgerald is interested, then its success at the Gate or Olympia is assured. In fact, it is the sort of play which would be excellent fare for the festival. If I can help to have it get a first class production, you have only to call upon me.

It should be pointed out in all this that Ireland had no official stage censorship while Britain had. Even as I was struggling to get this play into production in Dublin, Peggy Ramsay was writing to me from London saying that she expected trouble from the Lord Chamberlain's office on the play's content should it be taken on by a London management. By the time this actually happened, with Richard Eyre's production of the play at Hampstead in 1969, stage censorship in Britain had passed into the history books.

Jim Fitzgerald was the one who made the original production of the play possible. I got the script to him at RTÉ through a mutual friend who worked with him in television. Niall Tóibín agreed to play the lead and, suddenly, everything appeared to move very quickly. Fitz persuaded the sculptor John Behan to design the set and this led to another, lifelong friendship of mine, with John. Fitzgerald then brought the play to Brendan Smith, who accepted it for the festival.

Fitzgerald was an alcoholic and often flew by the seat of his pants. He was also a director of genius, particularly of actors in close, intimate, physical situations. In this way, he released a great, inexplicable power. Jim was also a terrific reader of text. He was a highly intelligent, well-read man who was subversive towards all conventional thought and practice. I couldn't have had a better director of my play.

I remember coming into the Olympia Theatre for an afternoon rehearsal, a week or so before the opening of *Mr Roche*. To my surprise, the doorman of the theatre, normally so welcoming and friendly, did his damnedest to keep me out. He offered some gnomic explanation as to why I shouldn't be in the theatre at this time. I managed to get past him and found the actors in a huddle upon the stage. Fitz was stretched out on the floor in the wings, completely sozzled after a liquid lunch that had gone on for far too long. The question of the moment among the actors was how to stop Brendan Smith from coming into the theatre. There was no problem about the rehearsal. They would rehearse themselves. The question was: How to protect Fitz? I was struck by the loyalty. Actors held Jim Fitzgerald in high esteem.

I don't remember how this all ended, but I do know that the incident was soon forgotten. Fitzgerald's production of the play was superb. He caught the violence beneath the surface of Irish male bonding and he made the difficult transition towards the end of the play with the 'resurrection' of Roche. He also got the play's comedy.

Brendan Smith was delighted with the stir that it caused. I was troubled by the hostility of some of the local reviewers. He dismissed them, loftily, as 'fleas on the back of a dog'. He also had his international success that year with the production of *The Cherry Orchard* at the Abbey, directed by Madame Knebel of the Moscow Art Theatre, with Siobhán McKenna and Cyril Cusack. That production was my first experience of the slow, stately, pictorial, Russian treatment of Chekhov, the whole action framed within quietness and repose. It was the beginning of my own fascination with Chekhov that was to lead, eventually, to my adaptation of *The Seagull* for the Royal Court Theatre in 1981. The Abbey production of *The Cherry Orchard* was not everyone's cup of tea, though. I remember saying to the writer Mary Manning how interesting it was. I should have remembered my use of the word 'interesting' to Mr Behan that night in the pub with Ben Kiely. Mary was one of the sharpest critics of Dublin theatre at the time. 'Interesting? Rubbish!' she declared. 'It's like directing the Lord's Prayer!' She became a friend.

My first encounter with her had been on that same opening night of *Mr Roche*. When the play had ended, I made my way through the stalls and discovered to my amazement that a number of groups of people had stayed on, standing about the place, talking about what they had seen. I passed one such cluster of women and was shocked to hear that they were talking about me. 'Who is he?' asked one. 'Does anyone know anything about him?' 'Oh,' said another, 'someone said he was teaching in UCD.' I slipped away quickly. Mary Manning was in that group. So was Shelah Richards. I was to meet them both, properly, shortly afterwards.

There was one other moment of significance on that night, shortly before I had heard the women talking about me in the stalls. This moment of revelation was created, appropriately enough, by Jim Fitzgerald. When the curtain had come down on the play, we were standing together, side by side, in the darkness of the wings. He turned to me and whispered in my ear: 'Your life will never be the same again.'

INDEX